ISBN: 978-0-9883247-0-1

Ido in Autismland

Climbing Out of Autism's Silent Prison

By Ido Kedar

Contents

Acknowledgements...7

Foreword...9

Introduction...13

Age 12, The Year of Anger and Sorrow..............................41

    Stims...42

    Impulsivity...43

    Internal and External Distractions..............................44

    Existential Issues...44

    Games and Distractions..45

    Motor Deficits and Other Body Issues............................46

    On Life Before Communication....................................47

    My Friend's Struggle..48

    On Faith...49

    Eye Contact..49

    On Being Silent and Liberated from Silence......................49

    Eye Hand Issues..51

    A New Optimism...51

    Apraxia Misunderstood...53

    Body Apraxia...54

    How I Would Have Liked to Have Been Taught......................55

    ABA Supervision..56

    Before Communication..57

    Stuck behind the Silence..57

    Overwhelming Anxiety..59

    Autism and Intelligence...60

    Letter Board and Keyboards......................................60

    At the Bottom of a Well...62

    Initiation Disorder...63

    Autism vs. Asperger's Syndrome..................................63

    How People React to Me..64

    Swirling Letters...66

    On Speaking Out..66

Empathy..67

Guessing Insights..68

Using Other People's Hands...69

Visual Processing..69

Blank Mask...70

Initiation Disorder..70

My Body Has a Mind of Its Own...................................71

I Wish I Could Talk...72

Test Validity..73

Mixed Senses...73

One Way to Prove I am Really Communicating.................74

Talking is Really Hard..75

Piano...76

Trust, Aura and Communication....................................76

Autism and Relationships..77

Why a Little Arm Support Helps...................................78

Shut Out of the Discussion..79

Sign Language..80

Proprioception...81

Liberated by Assistive Technology.................................82

"Theory of Mind" When it Matters................................82

Autism is a Deep Pit..83

Body Awareness through Exercise..................................84

Sad Families..85

My Start with the Rapid Prompting Method (RPM).............86

Remembering I have Two Sides.....................................88

Short, Long and Photographic Memory............................88

My School Education..90

Age 13, Starting to Let Go of the Past.............................92

Inspiration..93

Sensitive Senses...94

Fleeting Windows..95

Phobias..95

Games, Pretend and Theory of Mind..............................96

Bad Behavior...97

Communication Issues...98

Social Anxiety..99

Under-Estimated..100

A Kind of Paralysis...101

Language Processing..102

Recognizing Danger..103

The Curse of Self Pity and the Gift of Autism......................103

Hero...104

God and Suffering..105

Emotional Roller Coaster..107

Mainstreaming...108

Nature..109

Accepting My Illness...110

Overwhelming Impulses..113

Moses, Disabled Hero..114

Age 14, Motivation..116

Onward, Upward..117

Memory Triggers..118

Recognition..119

A Walk in the Woods...119

Emotional Overflow...120

Dogs and Autism..120

Autism and the Bossy Women...121

Noticing Our Blessings...122

Disabled or Super Able?...123

Sensory and Emotionally Overwhelmed by Well-Wishers........123

My Poetry Recital...125

Anxiety...125

Starting High School...126

Age 15, High School, for Bad and Good............................128

Nervous About Starting High School..................................129

Thanks to My Middle School..130

Autism, Other People and Discipline..................................131

The Hope-Fulfiller...132
On to High School...133
Envy is Lousy...134
Acceptance in High School......................................135
Letter to My Teachers..136
Autism and Friendship...137
Electricity in Autismland..138
The Lure of Stims...139
Autism and Adolescence..140
Sad in High School...140
Struggling Against Attitude.....................................141
Thickening My Skin..142
Lizard Brain...143
Starting Over..144
Special Special Educators..145
The Internal Autismland...147
Stims, Tics, and Freedom.......................................147
A New Chance..148
A Positive Change..149
Exercise as a Form of Autism Treatment.....................150
It's Not Polite...150
The Roulette Wheel of Life......................................151
Letter to a Friend with Autism..................................152
My New School...153
Getting Self Control..153
Non-Verbal Autism and iPads..................................154
Progress..155
Climbing Out of the Pit...156
Appendix...157
**Some Conversations on Autism betweenYoram Bonneh Ph.D.,
and Ido Kedar**...157
Glossary..164

Acknowledgements

Many people deserve thanks for making this book possible. First, I would like to thank my tireless mom and dad for their help, support, and faith in me. Thanks to many people on this mission are in order, especially to Leora Romney for her support and invaluable help throughout the entire journey, and to Roz Romney for her beautiful cover design. I would also like to thank Andrea Widburg and Sara Bildner for their input and help. I am grateful to Dr. Yoram Bonneh for his introduction and for our conversations exploring autism. Finally, a great debt of gratitude goes to Soma Mukhopadhyay for opening my prison doors and teaching me how to communicate. You made all this possible.

I dedicate my book to my Oma, Stella Better, who was my role model of cheerful bravery.

May, 2012

Foreword

I met Ido Kedar in the summer of 2011 and saw an intelligent fifteen year old boy struggling with what he calls "the stupid illness" of autism. Ido's observable behavior was exactly like that of a mute child with severe autism, with almost no eye contact, restless movement and self-stimulation, and "speech" made of unintelligible sounds. Yet, from his typing and a few other hints, I had no doubt that he was intelligent.

About ten years earlier, I was asked by Professor Michael Merzenich, a well-known neuroscientist from the University of California at San Francisco, with whom I did my postdoctoral training, to organize a group of scientists in order to investigate a fifteen year old child from India, Tito M., who, like Ido, could not speak, but wrote a poetry book with his own hand writing. He too, was severely autistic in his appearance and behavior, similar to the typical "non-verbal" or "low-functioning" autistic, as they are typically called.

Tito's case had initiated scientific discussion and debate, with some describing him as "one in a million" and an autistic "savant" for language. Because of this, I was anxious to meet individuals who are also severely non-verbal autistic, yet can tell us about this largely unknown territory. I thus met Ido and asked him many questions which he answered with passion, as if he took upon himself the mission of being a "mouth" for those miserable, mute autistics who are "locked internally, underestimated, and hopeless." But despite being very intelligent, Ido's skills do not make him a savant, nor a one-in-a-million genius.

Ido tells us that the main problem he struggles with is a problem of output. Surely, he has many other problems and difficulties, such as working memory and attention, sensory sensitivity and control of arousal and urges. Yet the main obstacle which prevents his true cognitive talents and personality to be expressed by his behavior is a problem of output—a severe disconnection between his explicit intentional conscious brain system and the automatic or procedural one, which is usually under full control, but in his case, so often is not. This claim is radically different from the common view that severe autism is associated with abnormal development of cognitive skills and a severe cognitive impairment.

Ido describes in his book several episodes that shed light on this tormenting problem. In one case he was asked to give flowers to his aunt. Since she was standing behind him, he could not see her and could not initiate any action to look for her, so he just handed the flowers to others. Ido, who unlike many autistic individuals has no problem taking the viewpoint of others, writes that this would typically lead his behavioral therapist to conclude that he didn't know the names of his relatives, and drill him with their pictures on flashcards.

On another occasion, Ido writes that his teacher stated, "It's clear he has no number sense" because his hands refused to pick up the right number of straws he counted, and he would "stand miserable and embarrassed holding the wrong number of straws." Similarly, he would open the door when asked to open the window or go to one room when asked to go to the other. He told me that in the past, when asked to choose from A and B, his mind would choose correctly, but his hand would consistently go to the wrong choice, making one think that he simply does not know.

Ido's descriptions are consistent with descriptions and observations made by other severely autistic individuals. For example, Tito, who could find a word in a page in a flash, was unable to search for an object in the room. Others are known to have poor motor control. Yet Ido analyzes his difficulty with the mind of a scientist, concluding that he must see something in order to move his body to get it.

As Tracy, Ido's mother, writes in her insightful introduction, therapists and clinicians were typically skeptical about Ido's communication and largely dismissed it as coming, although unintentionally, from his mother. I always wondered about the source of this objection, often called "clever Hans skepticism" after the 19th century horse that did simple math by picking up unintentional cues from his trainer. After all, humans are not horses, and they do possess the innate ability to develop language and high cognition. I think that the main cause for this resentment is that Ido, and other individuals with severe autism whom I have observed, show a paradoxical behavior, which may confuse therapists and educators. They may fail on simple tasks such as discriminating between two simple visual patterns, or answering a simple question, and at the same time write well-thought out essays. In addition, they may succeed in communication under certain conditions (place, specific aide, etc.) and fail completely in another, because of the peculiar nature of their skill acquisition and their neurological instability.

In the circumstances in which I observed Ido, he expressed his thoughts impressively, and provided interesting insights into his neurological condition which may help focus further scientific research. Reading this book, and my interaction with Ido, had a significant impact on my thinking, as it is not just a validation of other severely autistic people who write, but sheds light on the core deficit that often prevents intelligent behavior in the severely autistic. I am hopeful that his insights, so well expressed in his book, will contribute to the understanding of the severely autistic by parents and clinicians and lead to better interventions and treatment for those with his condition.

Yoram Bonneh, Ph.D.,
Department of Human Biology, University of Haifa

Introduction (Note: Ido is pronounced EE-doh)

Imagine being unable to communicate because you have a body that doesn't listen to your thoughts. You want to speak and you know what you want to say, but either you can't get words out, or what comes out are nonsensical sounds or the same embedded phrases you have said thousands of times. Imagine your face staying flat and blank when inside you are furious, sad, or wanting to smile in greeting. At other times your emotions—joy, anger, or sorrow—take you over completely and you have to ride with them on a frightening roller coaster. Imagine living in a body that paces or flaps hands or twirls ribbons when your mind wants it to be still and then freezes when your mind pleads with it to react. It doesn't enable you to gesture or write with pen or pencil, despite the fact that you read fluently. You lie in bed cold, wishing you could get your body to pull on a blanket. At other times your body charges forward impulsively, snatching things, or dashing you out into the street. Your body is like a prison and you don't know how to find a way out. Since you cannot express your thoughts, only you know that you are intellectually intact.

Imagine being stuck in an educational program, year after year, that is designed for a pre-schooler who learns slowly. You are bored, frustrated, angry, misunderstood and more than a little hopeless. You turn to repetitive behaviors, or "stims," which create a sensory drug-like experience that takes you away from the pain but makes the situation so much worse by pulling you farther from reality. You are lonely, though surrounded by people, and you know that this will be your entire life if you do not gain a means to communicate more than your basic needs. But no one is teaching you how.

Welcome to Ido's world. My now fifteen-year-old son, who has autism, emerged from this imprisoning silence after learning to communicate his thoughts by typing or by pointing to letters on a board. In these pages, he details and explains the symptoms and puzzling behaviors of his condition. He describes his life and education before he could communicate. He corrects what he sees as "erroneous premises" in much of autism theory and treatment and relays how he acquired communication and recognition as a sentient being. And finally he shares his point of view on life. This he does with humor, tears, occasional anger, and a bit of sarcasm. Ido's insights help us to understand life with severe autism. His story challenges our complacency with the status quo regarding autism education.

Beyond his insights on autism, though, Ido shares his story of personal growth as he comes to accept himself as someone who will always be different from others. The reader follows Ido on this journey, as his voice shifts from the rage and bitterness of an unhappy twelve year old, free at last to communicate burdens held inside for years, to that of a profound spiritual thinker making peace with his life. In this later stage, Ido triumphs academically, and in so many others ways, while studying a general education curriculum in high school.

Until he was seven, Ido had no means to show anyone that he was intellectually intact. His teachers and myriad experts assumed, based on his difficulty following instructions, lack of speech and odd behaviors, that his intellect and knowledge matched his actions. They insisted that the only way he could learn was by being slowly and progressively instructed in the basic information that human beings need to function. This would be done through drilling, flashcards and repetition for hours each day in a program known as Applied Behavioral Analysis, or ABA. While specialists held meetings in Ido's presence to talk about why he didn't progress on a drill, or how to improve his score on another, on the inside he was screaming, "I understand! I already know what a tree is. Please help me learn to communicate!" On the outside, the scream came out through his hands, vigorously flapping at the wrists. This was quickly redirected with the command, "Hands quiet." He was trapped.

Before Ido could communicate, I often had a strong suspicion that he understood receptively but that his expressive mechanisms were severely impaired. Unfortunately I had nothing more than glimpses or hunches to dispute the much more prominent evidence of his puzzling and impulsive behaviors. He followed instructions incorrectly and got simple answers wrong in drills. Moreover, the volumes of professional literature and expert opinion we sought all confirmed that autistic people like Ido had impaired receptive language skills as well as expressive language delays. Some experts stated that Ido was, in all likelihood, mentally retarded. Fortunately these expert insights were incorrect. Unfortunately it took a lot of suffering, time, and money for us to figure that out.

Most of the people we saw were caring and idealistic and a few loved Ido and were loved by him in return. Others, less so. However, nearly all were bound by a theory. They looked at autism in a theoretical box, as they had been taught, and this prevented them from seeing the true capacity of Ido and children like him. The initial presumption was that he was an empty slate who had to be taught simple concepts in slow increments. Many experts advised us that he was not even aware of the world around him. Of course, if one assumes that a child's vocabulary is limited to a tiny number of nouns and verbs, real communication is impossible. It's so out of reach it isn't taught. Some, in their certitude, refused to even explore Ido's communication once it emerged. They rejected it as impossible. They were not open to a new possibility, or as Ido says, they were "blinded by their professional biases."

Thankfully, this has changed for Ido. People who have met him cannot refute his abilities after observing him communicate without being touched or guided on his iPad or letter board. They therefore must either shift the paradigm in which they view non-verbal autism or see Ido as an isolated and unusual exception. For many individuals who have been taught that autistic children who behave like Ido are intellectually impaired, it is a stretch to accept that these children may in fact have sophisticated language abilities. It is challenging for those who focus on the clearly visible impairments to imagine that some of these hand-flapping, string-waving children might understand normal speech and think internally. Consequently, the response to the children who have managed to break through the communication barrier, and to their families, has not always been kind or constructive. Some have been accused of not being able to truly communicate, or being guided unduly by an overzealous partner (which may indeed have happened, but should not render every communicating child suspect). Or, since they no longer fit in the theoretical box, some children who have learned to communicate independently have been reclassified by the experts as not autistic after all. But, as in Ido's case, more often than not, children who emerge from non-verbal autism to communicate by pointing or typing are viewed as remarkable exceptions. It torments Ido that experts view him as unique while other children like him languish in silence. Through his book, he hopes to prompt the teaching of communication skills to countless non-verbal kids who are suffering as he did.

Fortunately, the communicative potential in non-verbal autistic people is getting harder and harder to refute. There are ever more non-verbal autistic people learning to communicate by pointing to letters and by typing, and some, like Ido, are going public. As with Ido, many of them are not touched as they point or type, which challenges the canard that they have been programmed to regurgitate their facilitator's thoughts. More and more non-verbal people are showing a different face of autism.

In the psychoanalytically-oriented 1950s children with autism were thought to have an emotional problem. The theory promoted by Bruno Bettelheim in his seminal work on autism, *The Empty Fortress*, and widely accepted by the professional community, stated that the "refrigerator" mothers of autistic children were so cold and rejecting that the children retreated into themselves as a defense against emotional injury. Hence the self stimulatory behavior, lack of eye-contact, and so on. The recommended treatment was psychotherapy and play therapy. Progress for the child using these methods was usually minimal and mothers had to endure being thought to have caused their child's autism. The data supporting this harsh conclusion was minimal at best, yet belief in it was widespread and thousands of autistic children and their families were affected by it.

In 1964, Bernard Rimland made the case that autism was not an emotional problem caused by traumatic childhoods and cold mothers, but was rather a neurological illness. The new theories stated that the illness was an expressive and receptive language processing problem, a severe social deficit, with other symptoms—excesses and deficits in behavior such as self-stimulatory behavior and impaired eye contact —that would be helped by intensive instruction, whether rote or more creative. The impaired outside actions reflected what was going on inside. Treatment emphasized capitalizing on the "window of opportunity" (we heard this phrase a million times in Ido's early years of instruction) in the child's early years to remold the brain so that the child might be able to appear normal in society. Children either were able to overcome their symptoms and become normal, according to this theory, or they stayed impaired throughout their lives.

All parents of autistic children hope that inside, behind all the impossible behaviors, exists a normal child struggling to get out. I remember being saddened to read from more than one well-respected source that this hope was foolhardy, that to believe this might be so was to be in denial, that parents needed to accept that behind their child's autistic behaviors lay an autistic soul. I read that what Ido showed on the outside matched his delayed inner world. Ironically, though I had been advised that there was no normal boy within Ido, our program was attempting to create one, or at least a facsimile of one, by drills and incremental learning intended to remap his brain. Hanging over us was the possibility that Ido might be one of the lucky ones who completely overcame all of his autism symptoms and was able to appear indistinguishable from his typical peers. Apparently it is okay to drill normalcy into someone, but it is denial to believe that a normal boy lives trapped behind a wildly uncooperative body. These theories cost us dearly.

Language is our pathway to connecting deeply with others. To be denied communication is to limit one to a life of frustration, loneliness and being misunderstood. Ido calls it "a crime against humanity." As Ido pointed out to me, imagine Stephen Hawking's life without his computer. Would the most brilliant physicist of our time be dismissed as a non-thinking person without this pathway to present his soaring thoughts?

I am a mental health therapist by professional background and spent years working with the Deaf. These professional experiences ultimately helped me to recognize Ido's ability to understand and communicate.

Like non-verbal autistic people, deaf people were viewed throughout history as incapable of understanding and even animal-like (this remains true today in many parts of the world) because of their communication impairments. The phrase "deaf and dumb" didn't come from nowhere. "Dumb" may initially have meant being unable to speak, but it expanded to being synonymous with stupidity. A lack of speech was seen as a lack of intelligence, and this "fact" seemed quite obvious in the past. Deaf people, raised without a language or any sophisticated means of communication, relied on gestures and grunts to communicate simple basic needs. Denied access to conversations, verbal social cueing, reading, writing, and full societal participation, their naiveté was assumed to be caused by impaired thought and not by impeded avenues to knowledge and information, or the isolation of being unable to communicate with others.

Similarly, well-respected autism sources state with certainty that about 80% of non-verbal autistic people are mentally retarded. Many of the non-verbal autistic people who now communicate at age-appropriate (or beyond, as in Ido's case) levels by typing or letter board were also once thought to be cognitively impaired.

An original thinker in 1700s France, Charles-Michel de l'Epee observed that in families where there was more than one deaf person, the deaf individuals began to invent and develop their own sign language system. He realized that through signs deaf people could be educated at a comparable level to hearing people. De l'Epee traveled around France, inviting parents to send their deaf children to a school he was establishing. Formalizing the home signs the students brought with them, de l'Epee created a systematic and more complex sign language that enabled the children to communicate all their thoughts at long last. Not only did de l'Epee discover that the children were not mentally retarded, he discovered that a good many of them were intellectually gifted. In Ido's case it also took an original thinker, Soma Mukhopadhyay, who found a new way to teach autistic children how to communicate through letter board and typing to finally lift him from his darkness.

Associating with deaf people showed me that speech is not a reflection of an intact or intelligent mind, but that the human being, if unable to access communication in the conventional verbal pathway must have another way to express himself. It also helped me to see that, much as there are distinct variants of 'deafness,' (profoundly deaf, hard-of-hearing, acquired hearing loss, deaf from birth, and so on) there are distinct variants of autism that should not be treated the same.

I spent a semester in college as an exchange student at Gallaudet College (not University yet), one of a handful of normally hearing students attending this Deaf institution of higher learning. I was immersed into a world where virtually no one relied on oral speech for communication. Students socialized, told jokes, participated in class, and gossiped with flying hands. The pathways to speech were inaccessible for many students at Gallaudet because they could not hear it. They saw moving silent lips on others and they could not hear their own voices. The majority of Gallaudet students chose to embrace their deafness and their sign language and to express their thoughts completely without the spoken word.

It was far easier for those hard-of-hearing, those with residual hearing, and those born hearing and later deafened to enter the hearing world of sound and speech. Indeed, deaf people told me how in the days when oralism dominated the education of the deaf, institutional schools demonstrated in public their most proficient speech readers and intelligible speakers, usually those born hearing but deafened through illness, or those with some hearing still, as evidence of the success of their methods. Many older profoundly deaf-from-birth people remain bitter about this, complaining that those success stories gave false hope to parents and unreasonable pressure to those deaf kids who did not have the advantage of ever having heard. Meanwhile, deaf kids whose speech was unintelligible and whose speech reading skills were poor lived in a kind of nether-world—unable to understand speech or speak well, but denied the use of sign language. The need to communicate compelled these students to learn sign language in bathrooms and dark corners, away from punitive instructors' eyes, who believed that sign language would doom the children to being unable to participate in the mainstream hearing world. The end result, however, was a group of people who didn't speak or lip read well enough to be fully integrated into the hearing world, but who were cut off from the Deaf community as well.

Two boys, both diagnosed with autism, may begin an intensive home program at the same time, receiving the same lessons, even having the same instructors, and yet one child may fly through the drills with correct answers and increasingly neuro-typical behavior, and the other, like Ido, may work his way through the same drills much more slowly, with much more frustration and much less progress. Is it due to cognitive delay, a deficiency in the child—as is so often hinted—or could it be a situation like the hard-of-hearing child versus the deaf child, where one has an innate advantage over the other in that particular system of instruction? When Ido was eight or nine years old, we were told by a specialist that we should accept the fact that he was not likely to progress much more. Certainly it was never suggested to us that he might blossom if we adopted an entirely different approach, by offering him a form of communication he could more easily access through typing or letter board. And so, the end result, so like that in deaf education, was that he was offered only speech, which was impossibly difficult for him; pictograms, which limited his communication to his basic needs; and an educational approach that waited for him to achieve what his body would not allow him to before he could move on.

Though both boys may have symptom overlap—poor eye contact, poor social skills and self stimulatory behavior, resulting in the same diagnosis, could it be that when it comes to treatment the differences are actually more significant than the similarities? Do the children have the same degree of fine motor control, body control and speech ability to start? Can one child follow instructions, engage in pretend play and limit his self-stimulatory behavior better? Can one child control his impulses better, anticipate events, initiate actions, and initiate communication, while the other boy does not have these skills? Shouldn't these differences be seen as at least as significant neurologically and in terms of treatment as the apparent commonalities?

When Ido finally got out of his "low functioning" autism class and was placed into a "high functioning" class, he struggled tremendously. His autism manifested itself so differently from the other children's. He was much more impaired in terms of independence, speech and self-control, but his racing mind flew through lessons that he had to wait for the other children to grasp. While waiting, his poor impulse control made him restless and disruptive, confirming to school staff his "low functioning" status. His "high functioning" autistic classmates had different struggles. As Ido observed, "They are not a verbal version of me and I am not a non-verbal version of them. It's something else, I think."

Not long ago, Ido was interviewed by a filmmaker with Asperger's Syndrome who expressed surprise, wonder, and even confusion at nearly every answer and explanation Ido gave to his questions concerning his life with autism. Later that day, Ido remarked that the two of them are generally viewed as being on the same spectrum, but it seems like they are dealing with completely different struggles.

Until recently only verbal people with autism could explain their experiences because so few severely autistic people had been fortunate enough to achieve the communication skills necessary to write books and articles. As a result, the vast majority of literature by people with autism has been written by people with Asperger's Syndrome or less severe autism. (Tito Rajarshi Mukhopadhyay, the son of Ido's former teacher, Soma Mukhopadhyay, was among the first to "break the silence" of severe autism with his first book in 2000). As a result, the professional community all too often has assumed that the insights of people diagnosed with Asperger's Syndrome or "high-functioning autism" reflect the experiences of non-verbal autistic people as well, differing only by degree.

In the literature, those with Asperger's Syndrome have often described themselves as having a social deficit disorder that can make them feel like outsiders or aliens, even feeling like they are observing human behavior in puzzlement, much like the character, Data, from Star Trek. In contrast, Ido has profound insights into people. His social impairment is not caused by an inability to read or understand human behavior, but rather by his body's refusal to listen to his mind's instructions. This denies him the ability to talk, communicate through gesture or facial affect, and control his sensory and emotional responses. The result is certainly a social deficit, but the origin is not due to Ido being unable to understand human behavior. The more Ido explained to me how he perceived the world, the more it seemed to me that so many of the books I had read by authors with so-called "high functioning" forms of autism, had not given me the insights I had hoped to gain into my son. Rather, their books had presented me with a fascinating glimpse into their neurological reality, which was not like his.

Every parent of an autistic child knows that once your child is diagnosed you have to become an expert very quickly. Since we got no guidance at all from the developmental pediatrician who diagnosed Ido, we immediately immersed ourselves in every resource we could find. We read, talked to people, tried to link ourselves with services and programs as fast as we could. Ido was two years and eight months by the time he was diagnosed—old by the urgency of remapping the brain standards prevalent in the literature and ABA. Hurry, hurry. The window of opportunity is closing. Soon it will be too late. Hurry, find a program, begin reshaping those neural pathways. It may too late already. Hurry, hurry, hurry!

For parents of an autistic child this is a daunting experience, and often you feel as if you are at the mercy of charlatans promoting the latest miracle cure—you just don't know what's legitimate, what's hype, and what deserves your time, money and hopes for your child. One source says that autism is a brain allergy that can be fixed by changing the diet. Another says it is a vitamin deficiency that can be cured by megadoses of vitamins. Turn the page, and another expert says the food allergy isn't in the brain, but in the gut, so the whole body must be detoxified. Other experts speak of a fungal disorder, and still others claim autism is caused by a hormone deficiency requiring regular hormone injections that may miraculously bring on the ability to speak. The next book promises that sessions with headphones that play music at unusual frequencies and rhythms may fix whatever is wrong. Many experts are convinced that forty hours a week of behavior modification drills, many using flashcards of basic information, may lead the child to normalcy. But the next book insists the opposite; don't drill the child at all. Follow his impulses and imitate him and his stims to engage him. Another approach advocates child-led play for a child who can't lead and doesn't play. Still another focuses on movement; he will calm in a swing and learn better. I was told Ido should swim with dolphins to rejigger the brain. And on it goes.

Each treatment has parents who swear by it.

Over time we looked into a number of different treatments and tried some of them with little to no real improvement. I had also read two books by mothers who stated that their autistic children had been cured by an intensive home program using Applied Behavioral Analysis (ABA), or behavior modification. Founded by Ivar Lovaas, Ph.D., ABA was logical. Teach the children with a severe learning disability what they need to know—receptive language, expressive language, pronouns, colors, labels, play skills, eye contact—in progressive little incremental steps. Motivate them with food and praise, just like training a dog; classic operant conditioning. (One of Ido's old ABA instructors actually WAS a dog trainer as well. She helped us to train one of our dogs to get used to living with cats and remarked that she was really doing the same thing as ABA). We also found a study that showed that a statistically significant number of kids who started early in the Lovaas ABA method had recovered. People observing them in a class with their typical peers reportedly could not tell which of the children had been born with autism and which had not. This approach offered us the hope of recovery from autism. None of the other approaches made such claims. Parents who had written books about curing their children through other methods—music therapy, diet, vitamins, imitation of the child—offered interesting anecdotal data, but only ABA seemed to have the scientific studies we sought. We knew what we had to do. Ido began an ABA program shortly after turning three.

ABA is an all encompassing program. It is in-home forty hours a week. It engulfs your child's life, your life and all your privacy. Since an adult must be present in the home at all times while instructors work with their child, parents are compelled to adjust their schedules to have at least one at home. Mothers or fathers may have to stop working for years at a time, putting careers on hold, or parents must stagger their work hours, rarely seeing each other. Parents juggle who will be home, who will work, who will drive the child to speech, occupational, and other therapies, and whether they can afford hired support. For parents adjusting to the diagnosis of their child and its ramifications, all this adds emotional and financial stress to the challenge. To make it through, parents need to forge a strong partnership of mutual support.

For the first three years of Ido's home-based program, my husband was the one who put his career on hold. All day long, little Ido was taken to the table in his room by instructors who came and went throughout the day, and asked to point to flashcards or stand up and touch his head or his nose. Some people told us that this was not a natural life for a child, that he needed the chance to play, to be a little boy. We countered that he couldn't play until he had the capacity to do so. Each drill, each reinforcer and each result was meticulously documented in a log book. It was scientific. It was all data driven. Some kids mastered the drills faster or slower, but they all followed the same premise, the same basic pattern of graduated building blocks. Once a week, all of Ido's instructors, Ido, and a parent would meet at the agency to review all of the drills and measure his progress. In front of everyone, Ido performed his drills while the supervisor watched the results and made suggestions to improve his performance.

ABA starts at the most basic level. Ido was shown two (later three, five or more) flashcards and asked to touch the correct one. In this way he was instructed in letters, numbers, labels (receptive and expressive), emotions, actions, people, colors, categories, and other indicators of his basic receptive capacity. For example, if the instructor was teaching verbs, she might hold up two flashcards, one in each hand, each with a picture of an action, such as a person walking and a person riding a bicycle. Alternatively, the instructor might place the cards flat on the table. (The number of cards put on the table increased over time as the skill improved). She would then firmly state in a high-pitched voice, "TOUCH," then add slowly, "walking." Then Ido would have to touch the correct card. If he did he was praised, "Good joooooob." If not, out came "NO!" strangely called a "neutral no" as it rang out in a detached off pitch. Neutral? Ido cringed each time he heard it. "He hates to be wrong," they'd tell me.

In this manner he was taught to follow simple instructions: to sit, stand, jump, touch his nose, over and over. He was drilled in eye contact, drilled in making increasingly complicated building block patterns. "Do this!" A script requiring him to put toy farm animals in a plastic barn "taught" him imagination. And all the while the instructors made sure to keep their faces a blank mask during drills, staring directly ahead zombie-like, or hiding behind a paper, lest they give any hints, glances or facial expressions that might give the answer away. To reinforce the learning, Ido had a plate full of treats broken into the tiniest quantities. For one or more right answers, a sip of juice, a smidgen of candy, a lick of a lollipop all quickly whisked from his mouth (he learned to eat and drink really quickly thanks to that), and later on for tickles and high fives.

A drill was either labeled mastered or unmastered. Once it was mastered, Ido could move up to the next level. For example, if he could make steady eye contact for fifteen seconds he could move up to twenty seconds. If he pointed correctly to all his flashcards he could get new words or even a new more advanced drill, such as categories. Until he was seven this was Ido's reality. Once he started school, ABA continued after school and on weekends. Though we didn't know it then, Ido was bored out of his mind, trapped in a paralyzing silence and frustrated beyond belief. He tried hard to show that he was smart but his hands and his body did not cooperate with his mind, so everyone assumed that he just didn't understand the concepts. I cannot imagine a greater exercise in frustration. "The experts," Ido says, "have no clue."

ABA worked on correcting the stims, impulses and the other excess behaviors we didn't want. For example, when Ido was young he flapped his hands a great deal. His instructors repeatedly and continually corrected him—"Hands down! Hands quiet!"—and taught us to do the same. Every moment, we were watching for autistic behaviors we were told to correct before they became habituated. Ido was incessantly corrected yet the behaviors persisted. He developed a fascination with letters, staring intently at the alphabet poster he had in his bedroom, staring at signs and license plates, dancing and flapping with delight with the credits at the end of a video or TV program. "He is fixating on letters," our behavior modification supervisor told us. "Take away his poster. Don't let him stare at letters." So we did, not realizing that our brilliant little guy, knowing that he couldn't speak, was teaching himself to read.

I kept thinking that some of Ido's behavior seemed to be communicating something non-verbally, though it was inconsistent and hard to interpret. Our specialists told us that he was too simple for that. Ido's first speech teacher told me that he was mentally retarded. "How do you know?" I asked. "Maybe he can't show what he knows and is merely 'functionally retarded?'" "It's the same thing," she said. The puzzlement for parents, the sort of cognitive dissonance in what we were taught was that Ido was assumed not to understand the most basic of concepts, requiring the most basic remedial and repetitive instruction. At the same time, his instructors covered their mouths, stared blankly straight ahead while waiting for answers at the ABA table, and avoided any glances that Ido would use as a prompt or clue to give the correct answer while pointing to his flashcards. In other words, he was assumed not to perceive ordinary concepts such as the names of basic objects or verbs, or to recognize human emotions accurately without drill instruction, yet he was considered to be hyper-perceptive to the most minute of facial cues. Which was it? Was he clueless or super-perceptive? Brilliant or slow? How can he, according to this theory, be both?

In another of Ido's treatments, Occupational Therapy (OT), which worked on sensory integration to help him with his sensory processing and body issues, Ido went from one swing to another—a fast spinning swing he clung to (we were told that autistic children did not get dizzy, however Ido proved that wrong by vomiting post session after a particular vigorous spinning by his therapist), a tight hammock, or a swing in which he could stand up, all with the goal of settling his vestibular system. The theory was that after swinging he would be focused and ready to learn. Though he enjoyed swinging a lot, these sessions did not appear to help his attention at all. Much later, we ealized that in spite of all the OT, Ido was in terrible physical condition.

Therapists spoke to me of his "soft muscle tone" but none worked on strengthening him. Moreover, his regulatory system had not improved. Years later, we came to realize that we had to concentrate on physical fitness, coordination, and body brain communication rather than on swings. It was then that I began working out with Ido. Ultimately, when Ido was about thirteen, we hired a personal trainer and a piano teacher for him to work on fitness, as well as gross motor and fine motor body control. For a child with minimal control over his body, exercise and piano lessons began to help him feel his body in space and to gain mastery over it, far more than anything ever had before.

Ido has always been prone to a high activity level and he could become downright oppositional, especially when frustrated. As a non-verbal child who supposedly didn't understand what people were saying and what was going on around him, he sure knew how to get people's goats. In speech therapy, when Ido was three, he was transitioned away from the "expert" therapist—the one who told me he was retarded— and began to work with a recent graduate from speech therapy school. Her sessions consisted of having Ido touch flashcards, just as he did in his home program, but with less energy, or verbally label the object in the picture, one after the next. This was too much for him. He hated it at home and he rebelled at getting it in speech as well, especially after a long drive. Ido began to resist and rebel, then to tantrum. He cried. He refused to work. The therapist kicked the non-verbal autistic pre-schooler out of her office.

I remember feeling so desperate as we went to the car. It was a feeling of utter hopelessness, and yet it passed through my mind that Ido did know what he was doing. How else could he communicate a logical frustration with a lousy professional? I scolded him, venting my frustration and embarrassment. Then I saw a clear look of defiance shoot across his face. He understands, I thought. But the look passed, the bizarre behavior resumed and every professional and every book agreed: He did not understand. He "sensed" I was angry. He "sensed" I was experiencing strong emotion but couldn't even identify what the emotion was (as was clearly demonstrated by the results of his flashcard drills on emotions). Nothing more.

So this was Ido's life. Pre-school in the morning. Forty hours of ABA a week. Speech therapy and occupational therapy and music therapy and other interventions we gambled on and hoped would work. Ido got older and he still couldn't speak, communicate non-verbally, follow instructions, or control his behavior. But we plowed on. The progress Ido made in his drills encouraged us, but he still flubbed simple answers. He appeared to enjoy his lessons less and less, scowling as he was led to his room.

In his essays, Ido writes of an experience that took place when he was about four, and I remember it well, when we sat on the sofa reading *The Jungle Book*. This was his favorite Disney movie. He had seen it dozens of times. Of course, as I was instructed, I didn't read him the story that he "obviously" couldn't understand. I asked him to touch pictures in the book instead, my hand lightly supporting under his arm near the elbow. "Where's Mowgli?" "Touch Ballou." And so on. Ido correctly answered each question. I remember the closeness I felt to him at that moment and I knew he understood. I knew that I had provided him with very light support under his arm that seemed to unstick him somehow, but I also knew that I hadn't been moving his arm or manipulating it.

When my husband, a scientist, came home I was excited. "He understands!" I exclaimed. I told him what had happened. I remember my husband's skeptical face. He asked the questions we had been taught by the professionals. "What happens if you don't touch him? Why would he be able to do something with support that he can't do alone? Do you think you might have been inadvertently prompting or manipulating him?" I didn't think so, but I was nervous. Ido and I tried the exercise again without me supporting his arm or touching him—this time with high stakes. This time his pointing was random. He hit none of the targets. "I guess you're right. He doesn't understand. I didn't think I was moving him, but maybe I was," I confessed. Ido writes that hope slipped away from him at that point and he died inside a little. I think part of me did too.

It took several more years for Ido to be able to show me that he was not the blank slate that we had been told he was. In the meantime, Ido went from kindergarten to grade school. As he grew his curriculum stayed the same. He started with 1+1 and several years later he was still working on 1+1. In the third grade he was still being shown ABC movies—the same one daily—in school. His teachers justified this curriculum because they were certain that this was the appropriate level of instruction for the children in the autism class. For example, Ido had trouble picking up the right number of objects when requested due to his motor control and body/brain communication issues. This was proof to his teacher that he didn't understand what a number was. Ido went from this "education" to ABA to other lessons. I hate to even remember those days. Ido hates to remember them even more.

At his best during those years, Ido was an affectionate, lovable and beloved child. At his worst, he was impulsive, passive aggressive (urinating in protest more than once), oppositional, unreachable in his inner sensory stim world, obsessive, and exhausting. We have a daughter. We have pets. The phone rings. We have chores. One blink, and down the drain goes a full bottle of mouthwash innocently left on the bathroom counter, or the new bottle of orange juice down the kitchen sink, or flowers casually get pulled off plants. I have friends of autistic children who have had to contend with children who in a flash became public nudists, self attackers, screamers, food snatchers. Or perhaps they have children who simply don't sleep. When there is no real communication, the relentlessness of these obsessive behaviors drives an exhausted parent to the brink because there are always the questions: Does he know what he is doing? Is this purposeful, or manipulative, or can he simply not control himself? Is there an end to this exhaustion?

With Ido, new stims came and went. He began to grunt when he was about six—a deep full throated, abrasive sound. It started as an occasional noise in response to annoyance, then it became a compulsive tic. All day, from the moment he woke up until he was finally able to fall asleep between the noises, Ido grunted every few seconds. He grunted as he ate, rode the school bus, and sat in class. It was maddening. All the ABA techniques backfired. Extinction (ignoring the unwanted behavior) failed miserably, as did direct command, "No" (neutrally) or "Quiet mouth!" The grunting went on for months. I yelled at him to stop. Nothing.

Then one day in my desperation I latched onto a radical idea. I would speak to him normally as I would to anyone else. Before driving I explained to Ido how distracting the grunting was and how it affected my concentration while I drove. I asked him if he could please try to control himself for the duration of the trip. To my amazement, he stopped grunting for nearly the entire car trip. My son, who supposedly could not understand, responded to normal speech and complex instruction. From that point on I was determined to speak to him normally.

We found a speech therapist who seemed able to engage him and to work more creatively on his speech. As with so many of the professionals who worked with Ido, she really cared for him. During sessions she alternatively hugged and kissed him, told him she loved him or reprimanded him for not trying hard enough. Repeatedly, she told him that he would be talking if only he tried harder and wasn't so lazy. Ido writes of the rage he felt in these sessions, unable to defend himself or to explain to her that talking was his greatest desire, and if it were just a matter of effort he would be talking, but that it was impossibly hard for him. Eventually, with no other means of communicating his resentment and frustration, he rebelled in speech therapy once again. He became uncooperative and grabbed his teacher's shirt and hair, certainly a non-verbal form of communication. The therapist's response was to send him home as unworkable. Once again, Ido's boorish non-verbal communication had liberated him from a situation he found intolerable.

The truth is that there is a big distinction between speech and communication. A parrot can speak but all it does is repeat the same imprinted phrases over and over. Deaf people may not speak but their hands convey their thoughts without spoken words, and we all know that just a look can transmit the most meaningful of thoughts. Ido communicated a lot in his outbursts but I don't think we always listened. We were too busy controlling the behaviors. Ido needed an alternative to speech. He needed a more accessible way to communicate his thoughts and he needed it right away.

He was finally able to communicate with me when he was seven as we worked on his birthday party invitations. It was like a miracle. Due to Ido's severe fine motor problems, at that time he was unable to write without someone helping him to hold his pencil. I had to literally place my hand over his to help him guide his pencil. Incidentally, some prominent autism professionals have disputed whether autistic children actually have fine motor problems. In Ido's case, these motor challenges have always been present. He has described his hands as being like "baseball mitts." To this day he cannot rip open a bag of chips or a candy wrapper. He needs to use scissors to cut the wrapper open. It took years to teach his fingers how to tie his shoes and even now his fingers struggle when he buttons or zips up his jacket.

Hand over hand, I asked Ido to write down words on his party invitations and I told him what to write letter by letter. B-I-R-T-H-D-A-Y. Then I told him to add in his friend's name. But before I could tell him the letters and spell it out I felt the pencil moving under my hand. He spelled out the word. I tried this again and again with other words without spelling out the letters for him. He spelled them accurately each time without me stating the letter out loud and without me manipulating his hand in any way. I knew I wasn't "inadvertently" doing a darn thing. I was supporting his hand, not moving it Ouija-board style. That's when I knew. I KNEW this time. Ido understood. He was not cognitively impaired. He knew what pronouns were. He used normal vocabulary that had never been taught in school or in flashcards. He could read and write. He had learned language the way every other child had; incidentally. We had all misjudged him.

I took out paper and talked to him. I was completely overcome with emotion, with guilt, with regret, with joy. We conversed for the first time in our lives. I apologized to him for misunderstanding and mishandling things in the past. I asked him why he never showed me before that he understood and could read and write. Slowly, chicken scratching under my hand he spelled, "I didn't know how to."

Ido had a lot of resentment because he had been so trapped. It was later exacerbated because no one initially accepted what I had to say. I had the feeling that all of our specialists in ABA thought that I had lost my mind. I remember calling our lead instructor, whom Ido loved, with our great, miraculous news that he not only understood, but he could read and write! Instead of responding with joy or enthusiasm, I felt a cold chill run through the phone. Speaking carefully, she told me that what I was saying was highly unlikely based on data and evidence. Moreover, she added, there was controversy in the professional community as to whether the children that were claimed to communicate at an advanced level actually were expressing their own thoughts. Ido was crushed at this lack of faith in him. For me, it was the beginning of the end of my patience with the wisdom of those who had guided the decisions about his education for so long. We lasted with our ABA program only a couple months longer. But this time I was not going to be deterred. I was absolutely certain that I was right and with certainty comes the confidence to stick to your beliefs in spite of hostile pressures. It was a very lonely time.

The constant doubt made Ido very angry. At last liberated to be able to express his thoughts and feelings, though in a facilitated manner, Ido was hurt and furious that those he cared for and who cared for him did not believe him. He was stuck with only his mom to communicate with, and boy, did he unleash a lot of anger and frustration on me. My husband, to appease his own anxiety and doubt, constantly tried to set up double blind tests to make sure it was really Ido communicating. "Tell Mom where we went today," he'd instruct Ido. "Ask him what we saw at the pier," he'd tell me. In these set-up tests Ido immediately became anxious and refused to answer, adding to his father's doubts. "Stop testing me," he'd scribble to his father.

But over time the incidental double-blind proofs mounted. Ido would tell me about something there was no way I could have known about. For example, one day Ido came home from school sobbing. I asked him what was troubling him and he told me that a boy, whom he named, had teased him on the bus. The next morning I mentioned this to the school bus driver and she told me that she would watch out for it. That afternoon when she returned she reported that she had caught that very boy teasing Ido and put a stop to it.

Moreover, Ido's funny, witty and delightful personality increasingly began to shine through his writings. When he was angry his writing was big and heavy, if he wrote about something sad he sometimes cried, and if the subject was funny, he laughed. Significantly, his ability to follow instructions improved rapidly as he continued to write. We went through reams of notebooks during this time, finally switching to a Magna-Doodle to save space and paper.

Because school was still miserably boring for Ido, we hired a private tutor, a teaching student who had no background working with autistic people, and she developed grade-level lesson plans for Ido in all subjects. He did well. It was almost surreal for him. He sat in school, learning nothing, looking at toddler books, adding single digit numbers, and at home he was writing essays, doing science, and multiplying and dividing double digits. Ido's tutor first learned how to support his handwriting through facilitation, and later she learned how to use the letter board with him.

Back at school, we tried to persuade administrators that Ido had a high functioning intellect that had an outlet in writing, to no avail. "No one," my husband, who by this time had overcome his initial skepticism, insisted, "will ever accept that it is Ido communicating as long as you support his hand." It was of course true. We began to search for someone who could help him learn to write without support. Miraculously, Soma Mukhopadhyay, who discovered a method she called Rapid Prompting (RPM) to teach her own severely autistic son, Tito, to type and express his thoughts, was living nearby at that time. A psychiatrist who was monitoring Ido referred us to her saying that she had had success teaching other autistic children to communicate by pointing to letters or typing. Unlike most parents bringing their child in to see Soma, I already knew that Ido could communicate. Our goal was independence.

Initially, Soma worked from her small apartment. A short while later she opened up her first private office. Ido was fortunate to work with Soma for more than six months before she decided to move her headquarters to Austin, Texas. The first lesson was like nothing Ido had ever experienced before. Soma, a tiny Indian woman in a brightly colored sari, began working him immediately. She showed Ido a grade-level appropriate science lesson in a textbook and began asking him questions about the lesson that assumed both his intelligence and his comprehension. Speaking at a rapid fire pace, Soma attempted to break through Ido's stims by taking his attention away from his internal and external distractions, and by verbalizing out loud the letters she wrote on paper and tearing the paper into sections. For example, Soma might ask something like, "Does a volcano erupt l-a-v-a, lava" (said as she wrote each letter down on a piece of paper which she tore off into a strip) "or w-a-t-e-r, water?" She then would put the two choices in front of Ido and he would point to one of the answers, without her moving his arm. Ido progressed from multiple choice to answering questions, to expressing his own thoughts. The first entire sentence he pointed on the letter board independently was "touch your nose." Soma read it, paused for a moment, and said in her hurried way, "No, no, no, no. We don't do that here." She told him that she would give him no food rewards, no breaks, and no rote commands. It was all about grade-appropriate learning and communication.

There is no question that Soma initially uses prompts often to draw out communication. This is a complaint I heard often by the professionals we worked with about her methods. She doesn't hide it. As Ido explains, her method *is* called "Rapid **Prompting**." Ido's ABA drills, school program, speech therapy, OT and every other educational approach he ever encountered was also heavily prompted. He was prompted to stand, sit, wipe his face with a napkin, look at people, stop stimming, play appropriately, master drills, and on and on. Consequently, I am puzzled as to why prompting every action throughout Ido's day was viewed by his specialists as an acceptable teaching strategy to be gradually faded, but that prompting Ido's communication (not speech)—also to be gradually faded—was viewed by them with real disdain and dismissed as manipulative. Because of this theory, some of Ido's experts who observed him with Soma when he first began working with her dismissed his early communication attempts, because, at times, when he froze, Soma placed his hand purposefully on a letter on the board to get him started. His teacher insisted that Soma manipulated Ido's pointing, though she didn't touch his arm at all most of the time, by touching his leg and giving him directional prompts that way. To this day I don't understand how that teacher thought Ido would find accurate letters on a board, spelling out complete words, and answering questions just because Soma's hand was on his leg. This, to me, is another example of the nonsensical super-perceptive versus tremendously delayed dichotomy in which many specialists view autistic children.

Ido's teacher and ABA home program supervisor told me that they perceived Soma as cruel because Ido resisted her when they observed him working with her. He initially scratched her hand and tried to bolt from the room because the work was so hard. But unlike many other specialists we saw, she persevered even when he had a tantrum. In fact, Soma had numerous scratches all over her hands and arms from students who resisted her initially in a non-verbal manner. It is important to point out how Ido feels about Soma. He states that she "saved his life," that she is a "heaven-sent innovator," and he is grateful that she toughed out his early resistance.

I remember the ABA supervisory session that was to be our last. My husband and I wanted to discuss how the program could best meet Ido's needs given the changes in his communication. Ido was not present this time but the entire team was assembled and all the young women were arguing, trying to convince us that Ido could not really communicate in the way we described. After all, they said, he had never communicated with any of them at this sophisticated level and the skill was not verifiable if it was not generalized with everyone. Moreover, the data from the drills did not reflect an advanced receptive and expressive ability. When we mentioned other autistic children they were aware of who communicated at an advanced level, we were told that they were probably influenced by their facilitator and it was doubtful whether they had actually communicated their own thoughts. When we mentioned Soma's son, Tito, who had been proven to communicate independently and was a published author, the supervisor replied that he was probably misdiagnosed, and was likely not actually autistic. When we brought up the possibility of eliminating some of the basic vocabulary drills from Ido's program, the supervisor impatiently stated, "It really doesn't matter whether Ido can communicate or not. It will make no difference in how we work with him." In other words, Ido would still be drilled in basic labels like door, potato, girl, boy, table and chair. That was when my husband and I realized that we were facing an ideological rigidity that was unable to adapt to the real needs of our child. It was scary to leave an approach in which we had invested so much over the years, as well as to separate from the team on negative terms, but their complete unwillingness to consider what we told them left us no other choice.

As Ido's letter board skills progressed, it became harder and harder to deny that he was communicating. Though we stopped providing Ido with ABA instruction, we continued to work with the same agency which has provided Ido with his exceptional one-on-one aides at school and with supervisors who are able to see and support his true abilities. To her credit, the replacement supervisor who came on board when we stopped our home program was able to see Ido communicating and to describe his skills as "irrefutable." She worked to help us get him into a more appropriate academic placement.

To support this process, I searched for a private educational psychologist who could assess Ido's actual academic ability, enabling him to communicate via letter board during his evaluation while she observed whether he was being manipulated or prompted. This was the first assessment Ido had ever had that enabled him to answer questions in his modality. As a result he soared from a low intellectual functioning score to that of an extremely bright child. The psychologist was utterly blown away. Over a period of several visits, she tested Ido's vocabulary, writing ability, math aptitude and so on. At the age of ten it was determined that he had a twelfth grade level vocabulary and his math skills were at least grade level (she stopped testing his math at that point because he was exhausted). As a result, in the fifth grade Ido was finally removed from his remedial autism class and sent to another school with a "high functioning" autism class. He finally had his first opportunity to receive an actual academic education in school.

Unfortunately, at every level this transition led to a very rough year. Ido faced a long school bus commute, skeptical administrators, and an abrupt transition into academic learning and the requirements of sitting quietly in a classroom all day. Worse was the loneliness, resentment, and anger he felt and expressed through his behavior. He used his letter board to communicate the most profane of insults and crude language. (We have no idea where he picked up this ripe language, as the raciest things he was exposed to at home at the time were Disney cartoons). During a vocabulary test, he embedded each test word perfectly in a sentence full of profanity, including: "I am manipulating this whole f%$#ing school." The only good that came of any of it was that the administrators finally could see that he was in fact communicating.

After graduating, Ido was sent to a middle school with a "low functioning" autism class. He no longer wanted to be the only non-verbal child in a verbal autism classroom. Plus, he told me, the instruction was too slow. He wanted to get an education but be with his autistic friends as well. The IEP committee (school committee which designs the individualized education plan for special needs students) agreed to mainstream Ido in the sixth grade in math and science and to give him grade-level academic work in all his other subjects. The autism room was available to him to decompress—a place where he could be himself with kids like himself, even though they could not communicate as he did. Though it was a lot of work, this was the best academic experience Ido had ever had up to that point. We were never made to feel that his intellect was doubted nor did we ever feel that his presence was merely tolerated. He was welcomed, and for this change in attitude we remain very grateful. In seventh grade Ido was mainstreamed in three academic subjects in large classes with forty-five students. With the support of his one-on-one aide he did the same classwork and homework as the other children and consistently earned all As and Bs on his report card. Based on this, the School District suggested that in eighth grade Ido should be fully mainstreamed in every class and thus be designated a general education student for his academic program. Now a freshman in high school, he is enrolled as a diploma track student and attends all regular classes for the entire school day, does regular classwork and homework, and maintains a solid GPA. He is scheduled to graduate in time with his peers. In this venture he is a pioneer. When I reflect that as late as the fourth grade, Ido had no exposure to a general curriculum in school because he was thought to not be able to read, write, or even to understand the simplest of concepts, I can only say he's come a very long way.

The ideas in this book challenge many assumptions long held by professionals working with autistic people. In our own experience, Ido broke free in spite of, not because of, the mainstream thinking today. If we had continued to rely on the specialists and educators who dominated Ido's early years, if he had not been able to find a way to show me that he could read and write, and if I had not finally trusted my own eyes and impressions, Ido would still be stuck as he was, locked internally, underestimated and hopeless. It is time for our understanding of autism to undergo yet another paradigm shift, and Ido, along with other non-verbal autistic communicators, is a pivotal guide.

The idea for this book was born by chance. At the age of eleven, Ido was asked to present a speech at a volunteer appreciation banquet for The Friendship Circle, a program that pairs typical teenagers with children with disabilities in activities. It was the first time he had ever been asked to share his thoughts in a public forum. It took place when he was in the fifth grade, which, as I mentioned, was a time of academic transition and great personal frustration for him. He wrote from the heart and described his experiences living with autism. The response was overwhelming. He got a standing ovation and was bombarded afterwards with hugs from people thanking him for what he taught them. Most moving was the weeping mother who told Ido that he had given her a window to understand what her autistic child experienced for the first time. He began to realize that he had an important message to share.

Some months after that, a psychologist Ido worked with asked him to share with her what stims meant to him. Ido sat down and analyzed his self stimulatory behavior. He realized that he could explain autism from the inside out, describing his symptoms and puzzling behaviors one by one. As he did, he began to understand himself better. He wrote about his education which then led him to analyze some of the prevailing theories about autism symptoms and treatment and how they affected his life. When Ido was twelve he wrote intensively. He was consumed with getting his message out. Nearly every day when he was in the sixth grade he would come home from school and write. Some essays were like a journal helping him to cope with the immense challenges he faced accepting his autism and attending a general education school. Other essays were intended to explain autism to others. As someone who could describe autism from the inside, Ido felt he had an obligation to help those with autism who could not yet communicate. He continued to write over the next three years.

Ido wrote each essay by painstakingly pointing to each letter on a letter board with me immediately writing down his words into a notebook. This was a slow process, but the words and thoughts here are his own, transcribed from his pointing. Rather than word by word dictation, Ido did letter by letter dictation. He wrote his essays in one draft. He composed and visualized his words before he pointed them out on his letter board. It was as if they were in his head waiting to be said. For me, it was a remarkable experience to be Ido's partner as he composed this book. With each essay I realized that what he was creating was a window into autism that was wholly unique and critically important. In many respects I was Ido's first student as he explained autism to me.

Many times Ido reacted emotionally to the topic. Sometimes he hopped up, flapped his hands, or paced the room, but he always came back to complete his essay. It was emotionally difficult for him to revisit the pain and frustration of his early years when he felt so trapped and terrified that his true intelligence might never be discovered. At the same time, the writing helped him to work through the trauma of this experience. To me, Ido's writing is not only remarkable for what it teaches us about autism, but also for the human story it tells of his own journey of emotional growth and self acceptance. His earlier essays can be painful to read. But the insights he offers into the experience of a young, intelligent, non-verbal child trapped by his body but mistakenly assumed to have cognitive delays and receptive language processing deficits, may help educators and parents rethink assumptions about how non-verbal autistic children should be taught. Ido's later essays reflect a young man who is finding a way to deal with the unwanted challenges of living with autism and to make meaning out of his suffering. Ido says, "I can't stim my life away." His is a story of the triumph of the indomitable human spirit. It is an inspiration to anyone who has struggled.

Although Ido's book was written via letter board, he has successfully transitioned to typing on an iPad as well. In the first sentence he typed on his iPad he wrote that no one would have doubt any more whether he did his own work or wrote his own writings. The iPad sits propped up on a table and, as always, Ido types each letter with no one touching him. As he types, each letter appears on the screen. He uses word prediction as often as he can to speed up the process. When he has finished typing he pushes the "speak" button and a human sounding voice speaks his words out loud. This is a great improvement for him over his old keyboard which he found cumbersome, with a robotic voice. The letter board is still faster and easier for him to use, but he is embracing the new technology in hopes that it will help him find his voice in the world.

We have been blessed to have some remarkable people support Ido in his endeavors. We owe such a debt of gratitude to all of these wonderful people. All recognize and encourage Ido's talents to help him overcome his challenges and function as normally as he can in the world. It is a relationship of equals. He is now instrumental in designing his own program to meet his own needs. Yet he is still far from "normal" on the outside. He still has his autism and all that it brings including stims, noises and struggles for self-control. But he is his own person now and he steadily triumphs over each challenge he sets for himself. He enjoys playing electronic games on his iPad and Wii, and unwinds watching cooking shows with his favorite chefs. He is achieving his dream of educating people about autism. He presents speeches at autism conferences as well as in many other venues. He has a blog, www.idoinautismland.com (from which some of his later essays come), and can be followed on facebook and twitter. He has been interviewed by medical students, autism professionals and filmmakers, and his writings appear in a book about autism. As Ido says, he has found his voice through his hand. And finally, he bravely continues to go to a regular high school, accessing his right to a normal education in spite of how difficult it is to be different and distinct, and to sit quietly and control his body. Ido's writing has helped him accomplish this. Ido wrote his first speech at eleven. Soon, he will be turning sixteen and completing his first year of high school.

I wish my amazing son success and all the power and strength he can muster to accomplish his goals and to live, as he often says, "a meaningful life."

By Tracy Kedar
May, 2012

Age 12, The Year of Anger and Sorrow

As I approached adolescence I was hit hard by sadness and frustration because of my autism and all that it kept me from doing. Though some of my essays are angry, I felt it was important to keep them in here because this is where I was emotionally during that difficult year. I had to work through the pain I felt because of all the years that passed before I could communicate. I also worked hard to understand myself and my symptoms better.

Stims

November 2008

Stims have a force that is powerful and compelling. They feel like forces that make resistance futile. It's like resisting hunger or sleep in some ways. They come into my mind so suddenly. Then I feel overwhelmed by the urge to do something like hand flapping, or noises, or spitting out water.

They work to let me release emotions sometimes. Other times they take over my emotions, like a frenzy I get on and can't stop well. I treat stims like a welcomed friend because they are really with me all the time. I am so needy to escape reality and stims take me to another world. I feel forces like waves of sensory energy. I am bombarded with silver lights and streams of color. It's beautiful to watch. They mesmerize me, but sometimes they scare me. Too many frenzied colors in my imagination terrify me. I am lost in the sensory world that is a relief and a poisonous prison.

Some stims merely amuse me like spitting water out, but others are a release from tensions. If I'm on a roll I find it hard to stop even if I need to. I listen to my impulses rather than the words of those telling me to stop. I like to be irritating to let my frustrations out. I know it's mean, but it's honest. I regret it later, once I've relaxed, but during the episode I don't have any compassion for how my behavior bothers others. This is because I am in my head feeling stimmy and words telling me to stop interfere with my pleasant high. Truly, stims are like a drug. I only have to lose myself in my mind and I am lost in a sensory world of big soaring feelings and wow, it's awesome. Then I have to return to my frustrating reality.

Stims are not predictable. They have internal drives I don't foresee. One day one stim is dominant. Soon another takes its place. I can't predict which will come but it's not hard to transfer to a new one.

I enjoy vocal stims the most. Other people hear those as pointless sounds, but for me they are entertaining. I hate the stims that take over my life like my former episode when I grunted non-stop for months. I couldn't stop even though I wanted to so much. It stopped on its own and I hope it never returns. I really had little control. It's much harder to stop stims when I am stressed. Then my self control is weaker. Sometimes I feel embarrassed by my stims when people stare. Still, I can't stop. Socially I know what to do but my stims never relent to permit me to alter my movements.

Hand-flapping is my most embedded stim. I started young. Today I still do it whenever I feel strong emotion. It's like there is a direct route from my emotions neurologically to my hands. No sense to it. I like the feel of it too. It is like a sensory stress release. To hold it in is like forcing me to not vomit; the urge is that strong. I don't think I would try to emotionally hold things in just to stop flapping because I would overflow inside. I know it's stopping me socially. It's a hard choice to make.

Mostly it's the reaction of others to my flapping that is hard to deal with. It's painful to see people react like I'm so strange to them. I'd stop if I had another way to release my tension. I hope that writing my feelings to others will let me free myself from flapping's hold over my response to strong feelings. It's not so pleasant to have everyone perceive my emotions even if I'd like to keep my thoughts to myself. Often they guess that I'm uncomfortable physically and it's really not that at all. Then I flap more from irritation. The "experts" mostly never get it right. They assume we are some autistic, retarded stim-machine, not a trapped, thinking person who has a shitty neurological illness. They need to limit our behaviors and stop the impulsive acts, I know. Still, it would be so nice if they realized how intact our minds were.

Impulsivity
November 2008

Sometimes I see something like a drink or food. It's not guarded so I take it fast for myself. People always get mad after that because it's so rude for me to do that. I feel remorse and shame later, but not at the moment I want the item. I am not sure I can overcome these impulses.

I know as I get older I ask too much of people to excuse my rudeness. I'm stopping too late in life. I know it's an important lesson and young kids master it. I bother my family when I do this by embarrassing them.

No amount of yelling at me will have an impact because the urge is without thought. If I think first, just for a moment, I might be able to resist. I find it hard to think first if what I desire is attractive to me. I need to work on this.

Internal and External Distractions
November 2008

It's hard to concentrate because my brain is full of distractions. If I try to do a game or a puzzle, it's hard to complete it because it has to interfere with my internal stim world. I am attracted to visually harmonious sights like water in the sun or lights blinking. These light my senses. I have to stop and look, it's so artistically awesome. Though I'm sure others can't see what I see and wonder why I stop, stare, flap to these sights, I see woven patterns of shapes and colors. No one who sees this isn't amazed at the lovely details of the lights.

I can't stop my senses. No one can. But mine overwhelm me. I hear my dog bark like a gunshot. My ears ring and I lose focus on my task. Tiny sounds are like soft buzzes I hear long after they have stopped. My hearing has advantages too. Boring lectures roar into street sounds so I tune them out. I can overhear interesting stories because I hear through walls in other rooms. Whispering is no defense. I have supersonic ears to eavesdrop.

Existential Issues
November 2008

Internally I'm so sad. I hate my situation in life. Is it fair to give a person a mind to think but no means to communicate with others? Is God good or is God indifferent to my pain? I wonder, is God ever going to help me?

Games and Distractions
November 2008

I'm not entertained by the ordinary things that most people enjoy. I endure what they love. I have no real reason to play games. I have no openness to games. I find them boring or almost like punishment. This is bad in a way because games are social. They connect people to each other, so my lack of interest is a big deficit. Usually I try to be friendly and stay a while but I have no pleasure. It's making my life more lonely because I am losing so many opportunities to relate to my dad, my family, and my friends. I feel sad when they try to play with me and I disappoint them, so I stim to escape my frustration. That makes things worse for them. Then I not only don't play, I'm unpleasant to associate with. It's a vicious horrible cycle. I've worked hard on play skills for years. I have to assume that I may not gain much improvement there because it's not interesting to me.

What I enjoy is music since it's a rich world of story in sound. I love instrumental pieces, especially classical. I would love if others listened with me. I like to walk, or scooter, or ride my bike. I need to move and to release energy kinesthetically. I love swimming, to jump on a trampoline, and recently to work out. If someone played with me this way, I'd try to follow. I can't explain why my senses prefer movement, but I'm resigned to it. I'm interested in cooking too, so I enjoy doing that.

If I'm on my own I retreat to stims. I can't stop this. I need support to stay engaged, so if I'm doing a puzzle or a computer game when the person who is working with me leaves, I will stop trying. That's one more situation in which I wish I could do better. I simply know that at this time I don't have the skills to stop my impulses. Time, I hope, will help, so I'll try to be optimistic.

Motor Deficits and Other Body Issues
November 2008

My body is its own challenge, all by itself. It's not only always restless, it's not coordinated. I have trouble doing basic tasks such as tying my shoes or tearing open a bag of chips. It's hard for me to do the tiny hand movements needed to write or do precise tasks. It's like my hands are baseball mitts or banana fingers. I feel so miserable that ordinary tasks are out of reach because it makes me delay my independence. My mind knows what it wants to do but my clumsy fingers don't cooperate. It's so frustrating to be twelve and to need someone's help to get my shoes tied. It reminds me every morning that I'm so disabled and often I become sort of depressed.

It's not just fine motor that is a challenge. My gross motor skills are slow too. I'm working out now to strengthen my muscles because autistic people have low muscle tone. I'm strong, but not fit. It's a lot like a car with a good motor but a leaky carburetor. I'm capable of getting in shape but I need to repair my deficits. In school we never worked on getting in shape. Adaptive P.E. is another formula for sadness.

I can't do coordinated movements yet such as shooting a basket or chasing a moving ball so I feel oppositional in adaptive P.E. (physical fitness class modified for students with disabilities). The expert teacher notices I can't do things so he tries to help me do things like a typical kid. The typical kid's got a working carburetor so his body responds to his instructions. Now the teacher tries to make me do something without repairing my carburetor first, so he pushes me to try. It's a big leap to throw a basketball into a basket if I struggle to feel my arms' positions, so I miss over and over. The expert tells my aide that I'm lazy and I feel so mad. He really has no clue.

The trainer I see is helping me to strengthen my body in incremental steps. I see my strength increasing and my coordination is also improving. He thinks first about my deficits before working on something. This means that I get stronger before leaping to a skill that is now out of reach. I'm so weary of experts that have no idea what the challenges of their students are. Instead they judge us.

I'm not sure where my body is if my eyes are shut. I must see my hands to know where they are. It's sort of terrible to open my eyes and see my body somewhere in space when I thought it was somewhere else. I see where something is so I can move to it, but sometimes I don't see where something is and my body moves to the wrong thing as if it had its own mind. Then I pick up the wrong thing instead. The result is that I robotically keep moving the wrong way, both to my surprise and frustration. I react in confusion because I can't understand why my body is in the wrong place. Time after time people assume that I don't understand simple words when they see me move wrong. Understanding is not the problem. It's that my body finds its own route when my mind can't find it.

On Life Before Communication
November 2008

The hardest part of autism is the communication challenge. I feel depressed often by my inability to speak. I talk in my mind, but my mind doesn't talk to my mouth. It's frustrating even though I can communicate by pointing now. Before I could, it was like a solitary confinement. It was terrible having experts talk to each other about me, and to hear them be wrong in their observations and interpretations, but to not be capable of telling them.

They misinterpreted my behavior often. For example, I remember that during my ABA supervisions, I sometimes ran to the window over the parking lot in an attempt to show them that I wanted to go to my car. What they said was that I was hyper and fixated on cars. They didn't understand how a non-verbal person might be communicating. Once, when I got really mad I urinated in my seat, but the supervisor just thought I couldn't hold my bladder.

But even worse was that they didn't support me when I began to communicate. Maybe they assumed I was too dumb, or they simply couldn't see what I had learned because I learned it in a different way than their methods. The response to everything was to give me drills.

If I had a dollar for every time I had to touch my nose, I'd be rich. I remember one day they realized that I hated being told to touch my nose, so they brilliantly switched the command to "touch your head!" I felt like a prisoner of these theories and methods in sessions lasting eight hours a day, forty hours a week, year in and year out.

My Friend's Struggle
November 2008

I have autistic friends who are not able to use a letter board because no one taught them how. It upsets me to see them so stuck. Have any of you ever gone to a country where you can't speak the language? It's awful to feel like you can't explain your ideas to anyone. For autistic people who are non-verbal they must deal with this isolation all their lives. Worse, is that too many people assume that autistic people can't understand because they can't speak, so they use baby talk or weird phrases like "go car" or "no big noise" to give commands. Inside we have a snotty retort, but outside we can only flap, or do another stim remedy to reduce tension. I am sure a lot of autistic people are smart like me, but they have no means to show it. It's not just speech. It's fine motor. It's body awareness. It's insurmountable obstacles that prevent the reply, so the autistic kid is treated like an unintelligent kid.

I see one friend in particular struggle every day to show his intelligence. His autism is even more severe than mine. His aide treats him like he is stupid. It's sad to see her and him together because she feels he can't understand or learn more. He is smart, I'm sure of it. I wish his parents would help him use a letter board but my fear is that they have accepted his limitations so they won't overcome them. My mom never accepted my limitations. To her I say thanks for rescuing me from my friend's prison.

On Faith
November 2008

I struggle with my belief in a good God because I'm so angry with Him.
No one who hasn't suffered can understand this feeling of abandonment
by God. It's one of the worst aspects of my situation. I'm forced to
doubt when I very much need God's love and tenderness. I know that
God is more than a wish-fulfiller. I understand that, but I wish now
to have God's love send me a cure. I wish for the strength to face my
trials. May God give me that, at least. I was urged to see God through
my helpers because they do God's work. I'll try to see it this way. It's a
more optimistic point of view.

Eye Contact
November 2008

Eye contact is hard because the light reflecting off the eyes is not
calming. It's hard to explain because I'm not aware that I don't look
at people until someone tells me to look at them. It's a strange habit.
I can listen better if I don't look at the person. I can look, but it's not
pleasant. In ABA I had to look in people's eyes with a timer. It was
so torturous I did it, but with terrible anxiety. I can't explain why. It
just is that way.

On Being Silent and Liberated from Silence
November 2008

Anyone can imagine being silent for a day or two. Can you imagine
silence your entire life? This silence includes writing, gestures, and
non-verbal communication, so it is a total silence. This is what a
non-verbal autistic person deals with, forever. Your hopes dim, yet you
persevere in going to ABA or Floortime (play focused treatment for
autism) or speech therapy, all to no avail. The therapists can't help
and you despair, and only you know that your mind is intact. This is
a kind of hell, I am certain.

The experts focused on stim management, or drills of rote activities, or silly play like finding things in Play Doh, over and over, on and on. But they never taught me communication. I shouted to them in my heart, "I need to communicate!" They never listened to my plea. It was silent.

I could read from an early age. I could write too, only my fingers were too clumsy to show it. In school I sat through ABC tapes over and over and added 1+2=3 over and over. It was a nightmare. I was bored out of my wits. It made me die inside. I was like a zombie inside because I had no hope.

I had a change when I was seven. My mom sat with me doing birthday invitations for my party. She supported my hand so I could write. I did spelling under her hand. She could feel it moving independently and realized it meant that I could write. We wrote together. She cried and apologized for not knowing sooner. I was angry and swore and insulted her. We wrote often then and it was a relief, but my life didn't change. No one believed us at all. My ABA team tried to convince my mom that she was wrong. This hurt me so much because I thought they'd be happy for me and teach me how to communicate better. Instead I stopped working with them. School didn't change. My teacher was skeptical. It stank because I endured doubt on top of boredom. At first, my mom couldn't even convince my dad, the scientist, so it was lonely. My mom bore the brunt of my frustration. I was full of anger because I could only communicate with her.

Then, we found Soma. She saved my life. She talked to me like I was smart. She taught me how to communicate in steps. She is an angel, I think. I am eternally grateful to her for her help. My teacher and ABA supervisor observed me with her and saw only prompts. They refused to believe in me. I hated them too. I was full of rage then. I hate to remember that dismal time. But gradually my independence improved and the skepticism started to fade in my dad, my supporters in school and others too. Now people know I am intelligent and a unique person. I thank my mom for seeing the truth in me and for my dad in opening his eyes in a scientific way too. I am so fortunate to have them to guide me through this strange world as a silent boy no more.

Eye Hand Issues
November 2008

I have to learn to use my eyes at the same time I use my hands. I often use my hands or my eyes to do things. It's hard to explain. There are some activities in which both work together. For example, if I ride my scooter they are a team. My eyes see and my hands move the scooter. Same with my bicycle, but when I need to change my clothes I feel my way. If I look, I get flustered. The result is that I often dress carelessly. My shirt is on backwards and my sock is heel on top. My mom says, "Look at what you are doing," but I can't seem to figure out how.

The difference between pointing on my letter board and doing these tasks is that pointing is communication. I want to communicate so much that I am able to overcome this deficit. I have to look when I point or I'm silent. I'm more motivated to try. This is also true with my scooter, which is fun. But with other activities it's tough to get my eyes and hands to work together. I don't feel especially motivated about my socks so the skill can't improve. I know this interferes with my independence so I should care, but I get no immediate pleasure from it. I don't work well for goals ten years from now. I never really analyzed this before. Only I can change this. If I cared I'd try harder.

When I cook I have to look. I love to cook so I do. It's the same principal. If I care I look and try harder. If people tell me to look when I am doing something I hate, like my dumb socks, I tune them out. It makes my mom angry to tell me to look year after year because she wants me to be more independent. It is a new concept if I do something for the future and not my immediate gratification. It's a more mature idea too. I need to think about this more.

A New Optimism
November 2008

Last night after Thanksgiving dinner it was hard for me to stay engaged in social activities when we played outside at ping pong and Taboo, but people accepted me and really welcomed me. It was a lot of fun yesterday. I really enjoyed the playing. That's new for me. I saw that the games were not a test of my play skills. They were just meant to be for fun. It was great to do so well in Taboo. People could see I am very clever, just not good at speaking.

It's frustrating to try to play with the kids my age. I'm better off with adults. Adults accept me and welcome me. I'm more intellectual than playful. Only if normal kids find a way to respect me, I relax some around them. Some of the kids who were there are better than before, when they ran from me and wouldn't sit near me in a car, but they don't exactly want to play with me, so I decided to quit suffering inside, to stop trying to hang out with people who don't want me there and to join the ones who do. It was the best decision. It really helped me to have a great time. The adults were so cool. Some were young, out of college or still in college, others older, but all of them welcoming. Often I anticipate rejection, but it never came. I'd love to have more nights like this. It was so heart-warming. I got a taste of how much better my life can be if I stop destructive self-pity and engage with respectful people. I'm a good person to know. I should be proud of myself, not bitter. I shouldn't isolate myself. I'm sad to think how much time I've wasted in self-pity, but I see it's a decision. Last night I could have felt that, but I chose not to let myself go there. I'm aware now how much I made things harder for myself. I know it won't be fun in school or all the time, but I believe that I can get over my self-pity to lead a full and happy life.

It's do-able. It's possible to have a normal holiday in spite of the limits of autism. I never isolated myself, or disappeared in my head, or felt down, or compared my situation to the typical kids. I normally did all of that so I'm thrilled I found the fortitude to try all weekend. Thus begins my more optimistic phase. I'm determined to take November's Thanksgiving as a model for trying to relate to people in play. I believe it's a start on a new road. I don't see myself going back to my old lousy path. I'm done with it. I need to remember that people accepted me, not in a pitying way, but as part of the group. It's a great feeling.

Apraxia Misunderstood
December 2008

It's hard to speak because apraxia is like a bad phone connection. I know my thoughts are getting lost on the way to my mouth. I think of an idea. I try to say it and the wrong thing comes out. For example, I might really want to get a chicken dish for dinner in a restaurant, but if someone asks me if I want beef my mouth is often messing it up by saying "yes." It's so frustrating because I suffer through getting the wrong meal even though I responded to a question. It's like my mouth is surprising me and I have to obey it. If it's not a yes/no question it's harder. It's like my thoughts don't get out at all. I have phrases I've memorized, but it's not even close to my actual thought. I might think about a baseball game and say something like, "cookie" or "tickle." I get irritated by my inability to get my thoughts out. It's the most horrible aspect of my autism. It's the loneliest thing you can imagine. If I could change it, I'd be so happy. It's my hardest frustration by far, and that's saying a lot.

It's not easy to overcome this problem. I was in speech therapy for many years. I never progressed more than a little. Overcoming my speech deficits requires that my brain is able to send messages to my mouth and it forces me to drill in my mind new neural pathways. If you think that's easy, try writing with your mouth or your foot. It sounds funny, but I think it comes close to what speech therapy is for me. I've had speech therapists who don't understand how hard it is. They get irritated if my progress is slow. I had one teacher who scolded me and told me I was lazy. She was sure I couldn't speak because I didn't try hard enough. I did try, but it was hard. The lessons didn't flow in progressive steps. I couldn't keep up with her exercises and I couldn't speak in my own defense. I think if the experts could live in my body one day, they could understand much better. They mostly mean well, not harm, but intentions make no difference if they misread my behavior, and unless there is communication in two directions, there's a big risk of that happening. Unfortunately, we can't have communication in two directions if they don't teach us to communicate in a modality we can do.

If I had to stick with only speaking I'd be stuck internally, maybe forever. I don't understand how the experts don't realize this. Even if I show them how I communicate, they persist in seeing me as an isolated case and don't help other kids communicate like I do. I don't understand why this idea is so tough for them to generalize. Maybe I need to use the same flashcards they used in my generalization drills on them. Ha ha. I've even suggested directly to some experts that they should teach letter board to their students. I've told some of my friends' parents too, but it seems that they can't believe the other kids have it in them. Of course, everyone doubted me too before I proved myself.

If my book does one thing I hope it helps get non-verbal autistic people more communication. Soma deserves an award for her insights. She is a true innovator. I'm grateful to her. I know she is doubted by the experts, but maybe they are experts with books and diplomas, not insight. Soma is insightful. She gives non-verbal autistic kids hope. That's a blessing because too often my experts brought me only desperation. I may never overcome my apraxia but I'm not trapped in silence, thanks to Soma.

Body Apraxia
December 2008

I understand everything but sometimes my feet interfere with my thoughts. It's like apraxia in my body. I want to say "no." My mouth says "yes." I want to go to my parents' room. My feet go to my room. This is a terrible problem because then people assume I don't understand basic information. It has happened so many times over the years.

It frustrates me to look back at how my ABA teachers drilled me endlessly in basic skills only to say it wasn't mastered because I had inaccurate pointing. I knew everything so easily. I was bored to tears but my apraxic hands would go to the wrong card so they thought I didn't know "book" or "tree." I did it over and over. It was the worst. The assumption that people don't understand if they reply incorrectly is a huge misconception. ABA is built on this erroneous premise.

My ABA teachers would talk baby talk and tickle me to reward me. I cared that they see me as smart, so I tried, but I think it was pointless. I often felt that they couldn't see my potential, just the drills. I feel it's time autistic people finally said what it's like to be drilled in flashcards over and over when your hands don't move to your thoughts, or to have your teacher say in front of you that you can't count because your stupid hands refuse the right number you've counted in your head. I remember standing miserable and embarrassed, holding the wrong number of straws and hearing my teacher say, "It's clear he has no number sense," as if I couldn't understand or had no emotions either. When I think of these frustrating experiences I am grateful I am not in that situation anymore. But many of my friends still are. That's why I cry for them. Go and teach them to communicate. I wish that all non-verbal autistic people would learn to communicate too.

I point accurately on a letter board because I try so hard to communicate. It's a skill that's helped me to overcome much of my hand apraxia. I can do much better now with counting things like forks or knives when I set the table, or if I write on paper. It's a telling thing that my hands mostly are accurate in communication which is my most heartfelt desire.

How I Would Have Liked to Have Been Taught
January 2009

I was asked how I would have preferred to have been educated in my early years. If I could educate the specialists the first thing I'd recommend is to talk normally to autistic kids. No more "Go car," "Close door," "Hands quiet," or the like. It's stupid to talk this way. Some teachers used tones to make words more distinct or spoke slowly or in over-enunciated sounds, like "letter" made with a "t" sound, not a "d" sound like we use in America. They sounded so silly I often rolled my eyes inside. So that's my first suggestion.

Next, I would teach autistic kids grade level lessons so that they learn the same stuff as normal kids. You can't imagine how boring it is to be drilled over and over on baby tasks that you know but can't get your body to show. The specialists need to teach, not just drill. I love books and would have enjoyed some age appropriate stories, not baby picture books over and over. So, even if they think the kid doesn't understand, they shouldn't deny them interesting lessons.

The next suggestion I have is to teach exercising that is designed to give kids more communication between body and brain. In OT (occupational therapy) it was fun to swing and climb so I liked going, but it didn't help me to be more fit or to regulate myself. If I had worked on fitness, muscle strength, or steps incrementally working on body control it would have helped more.

Speech therapy is important so I'd recommend it; still, it's not enough for non-verbal autistic people. They must also have communication. To deny communication is a crime against humanity. It is cruel in result if not intention. I was helped by Soma's techniques. Others may be helped by her techniques as well, or by other methods, but to deny non-verbal autistic people a voice is wrong. PECS (Picture Exchange Communication System) is not enough. It's so basic. Sign language is impossible for people with fine motor deficit and hand apraxia. Letter boards offer full communication and are easier to master for hand apraxic people. Soma is the greatest teacher of autistic people ever. She rescued me from isolation. The sad thing is that she is treated with scorn by so many leading experts who are too much invested in drills and rote learning to see our need for communication now. I wish I could convince them, but I doubt it. If I could influence a new generation of teachers and parents I would be thrilled.

ABA Supervision
January 2009

In ABA supervision I had to do drills in front of a supervisor with all my teachers. Then they'd talk about me in front of me to decide how to improve my performance. It's miserable to be an object of study especially because they never realized I understood what they were saying. The consequence of testing me in front of people is that I grew embarrassed and ashamed inside. By analyzing me in front of me, usually wrong, I grew resentful. It was so frustrating I don't like remembering it to tell it now. It's over for me, thank God, but not for other kids so I have to share this to help them too. My advice is that it's important not to discuss the child in front of him like he can't understand or has no emotions. Try to imagine what it feels like to be in that situation week after week.

Before Communication
February 2009

Before I could communicate I was often there in body but not in spirit. I understood most things but I knew I was trapped and could not show I understood. It forced me to stim more because I had to live inwardly. Even if I thought about interesting ideas, since I couldn't share them it was pointless. Once I had communication my world opened. If I had interesting thoughts I could tell my mom, or my aide, or Soma, or my tutor, or my mom could tell people what I wrote. This made me hopeful and interested in learning more.

It's really miserable not to have communication. It's so awful it's hard to explain to someone who can talk, gesture or write because a non-verbal autistic person can't do any of these things at all. It's like living behind a wall of isolation. I survived by stimming or TV or hugs from my loved ones, but I became me once I could express thoughts and connect intellectually to others. It is awful to remember those days so I'm stopping now.

Stuck behind the Silence
February 2009

When I was very young I didn't know I was different. Later, I noticed when I tried to respond that I couldn't talk or gesture. I was still a little kid but I could see that I didn't act the same as the other kids.

I know people don't believe that a little kid notices, but I did notice. I'm more aware than most because I observe so much. If you can't talk you have to notice things or you go nuts. I heard my parents converse about me and their worries. I heard the professionals diagnose me and talk about me. I heard the predictions for me and the weekly assessments. It mostly interested me. I heard everything but I knew that only I knew my real situation. Inside I shouted my story, but outside I only flapped in frustration. Then they told me, "hands quiet" or "hands down." Like I mentioned before, each day the experts denied me hand-flapping but I had no other outlet for my feelings. What else could I do? I couldn't talk, write independently, gesture, or initiate. It was hard to endure this, but I was totally stuck with no way out that I could see.

It's hard to describe this time well. I did impulsive things that I couldn't explain and people got angry at me. It was awful because I understood why they were mad or exhausted but I couldn't stop the naughty behavior. This is why communication is so essential. No one should be unable to stand up for themselves. During these years I felt so trapped. Many times I felt like killing my dumb self and being free of this hell. I never would and I've overcome this feeling now. I'm intent on living. I appreciate that I have a wonderful family, a good home, friends, and three dogs too. I get lots of love and support. I believe it will get better. I'm not without hope now, but I once was.

In ABA years I lost hope. I'm telling this for the first time. I longed so badly to be able to make my ideas known. I got flashcards instead. Though I liked the teachers as people, I feel I wasted many years in this lonely endeavor. "Touch your nose." "Touch tree." "Touch your head." "Look at me." "Do this." "Sit quiet." "Touch red." "Good job." "Hands quiet." "No." "Great." "No." "All right!" "No."

Soma didn't do any of this. She gave me no reinforcers. No food. No tickles. Just normal communication in pointing. Wow. I'm telling you it was like being born into me. I told jokes. I wrote stories and plays. It forced me to try to communicate, to get an education, to be part of the world. Before, I felt like a lab rat running in their maze of flashcards but not finding an exit. It took Soma to open the door. I didn't know how to do it alone.

My life is better now. I'm having fun in gym, piano, exercising, books, nature. I'm communicating with more and more people now. Though I still get sad, it's true, I'm not hopeless. Now I'm living in a flashcard-free world. I'm never touching my damn nose again.

Overwhelming Anxiety
February 2009

I saw a neurologist who said she thinks autism is a severe form of anxiety disorder which inhibits our ability to respond. I have been thinking about this idea. I think there is truth to it. It's obvious to anyone who spends time with an autistic kid that we are always anxious. Some kids even hurt themselves. In one case I see a boy hit his head and bite his hand. In another, I know a boy who yells, "I've got to get out of here!" often. I see kids flee and flap and cry and scream. They have no good outlet for strong tension so anxiety is a symptom of autism, I'm sure.

I also am anxious with people. I trust few completely enough to use my board with them though I may enjoy being with them. I'm anxious with kids especially because they often are staring at me or impatient. Their high energy also stresses me out. I feel my body tense up instantly when kids who are yelling in play enter a room. Then I only want to flap or pace to calm down. I think the doctor may be on to something. I realize I am anxious twenty-four hours a day. Sometimes I can manage it and sometimes it overtakes me. The problem is that my anxiety can be like a form of paralysis. I can't speak or move to my thoughts so it interferes with my life terribly. Then people misunderstand my behavior.

I saw yesterday that an autistic friend of mine trusted my mom. She talks to him with understanding and respect. He has less verbal ability than me so he is so stuck. I saw him learn to trust my mom over weeks. Yesterday she used my letter board with him. He wrote with her. It was awesome, but I saw doubt on his mom's face. So did he. Whenever his mom looked, his hands stopped cooperating, so of course she doubts more. This is a curse. When you need to show your skills, anxiety hides them. Then people conclude that we don't have them or, at best, are being manipulated.

Anxiety is the source of much of my failure in social situations and in public. It overwhelms me so much I flee or withdraw in my stims or in front of TV. It is one of the reasons I am so shy. It's not a lack of knowledge or awareness of others. I don't think a person is an object like some experts claim. I just can't relate when my anxiety is overpowering me. So this is one request to all researchers: start looking into anxiety. I think it may be a key to solving the riddle of autism.

Some treatments increase anxiety, especially hand-anxiety in my case. To this day if I behave badly I wait for the "neutral no." I imagine if the behaviorists all heard "neutral no's" all day long each time they did something wrong it would make them edgy and tense and they would start to flub in their nervousness, especially if it started when they were two years old. So I am realizing that some treatments make anxiety worse.

Autism and Intelligence
February 2009

I don't really understand the link between autism and high intelligence but it is obviously there. It is not coincidence that so many of us have smarter than average families. It's worth some research into this. It's like there is a high intelligence mutation or something coupled with a high anxiety mess-up. The irony is that we seem dumb but are often a lot smarter than average, but since we can't express our thoughts we have to endure lessons in school that would bore a three year old.

Letter Board and Keyboards
February 2009

The letter board is the easiest modality at this time for me to use in communication. It's fast and it's not as precise as a keyboard so it's easier for my fine motor skills. I struggle with keyboards because I have to concentrate so hard on the small keys but I do it because I want to become more independent so that it's clear to everyone that I do all my own writing. Because of autism's paralyzing anxiety and distractibility it helps a lot to have someone I trust near me to keep me focused. I think it's clear to most people now even if I use a letter board that no one moves my hand or the letter board. I think it's hard to deny that it is really me communicating at this point but I know I can't convince everyone except open-minded people. I have company, like Columbus, Galileo and many others who were doubted in their time and later proven to be right. It's not my job to convince skeptics. I just need to tell my story. If they have doubts, so do I, about their judgment. They are missing the true story because they see everything through their theories.

Some will ask why I need someone to hold my letter board. I don't. I can use the keyboard on the table. It's a lot harder, slower and more stressful. The letter board at eye level is hemming in my distractions. So is the person holding it who helps me stay on track if I try to flee or lose focus. This is necessary because I get up often.

Trust is an important part of communication too. I need to trust the person who helps me or I get very anxious. I won't write with someone who is skeptical or treating me with idiotic patronizing baby language. Too bad because that's most autism experts.

It's almost a joke to me that some people worry if someone holds up my letter board for a conversation. That's too invasive a prompt, according to certain theories, but saying "Hands down," "No," or "Do this," are fine. This is a kind of educated blindness.

The theories go on as they do until a new one takes hold. Look at Bettelheim's theory. My mom told me she likes to keep his book, The Empty Fortress, to remind her that trends in treatment come and go and he was wrong, and for my autism a lot of the theories people believe today are also wrong, in my opinion. Do I sound angry? Well, I am. It's time autistic people told the experts that they have made mistakes. It's time we told them "No."

At the Bottom of a Well
February 2009

I am lonely in school. So are my autistic classmates. We could laugh and tell jokes and have fun if they could use a letter board. It makes no sense to me why they are not taught it. It's not nice for them to see me communicate and to be denied the same opportunity. Why is the world so cruel to them? One of my classmates had a taste of communication with my mom and now he is silent once more. I see he watches me in sadness. It hurts me to see it.

I'm talking to all you parents now. You need to let your kids communicate in their way on letter boards, keyboards, or any typing device. They will need your support, your love and your belief in their intelligence to succeed. I think autism is like a solitary confinement. Communication can't be accessed without help and the right kind of instruction.

It's like a well. The autistic person is stuck at the bottom and needs to climb out. The trouble is how. The autistic person can't initiate the escape. It's not from a lack of desire. It's hard to explain. I don't know why we can't initiate typing. I wish I could have, then I would have been able to tell my mom that I was smart so much sooner. My friends in school still can't tell their parents. It's a tragic situation because the kids need to communicate. Their moms and dads want so much to talk to them. They love each other but they are separated because the kids are in the well and the parents stand on the top. Pictograms aren't a ladder. They are a stepstool. The way out is in real communication, not in basic needs communication.

It is true, these autistic kids stim and seem odd and get things wrong often. These are all symptoms of autism. Nevertheless, they are no different than me. It's due to my stubborn mom and my luck in meeting Soma that people see me now as intelligent and even different than my autistic friends. If my mom had not discovered I could write I'd be down the well still with them and without a ladder. I cry inside all day to see my friends down the well. They deserve Soma's ladder out too. There is a way out. I may be far from normal. I'm still very autistic. I stim and am impulsive and am not very verbal. I am anxious and shy too but I am a free soul because I can communicate my thoughts to the world. I wish this for all autistic people.

Initiation Disorder
February 2009

I can't explain some aspects of my autism. I don't know why initiating is so hard. I may wish to say something or do something. I can't get myself to move on it. I'm too slow in my reactions.

I'm hot. I keep my sweater on. I'm cold. I don't put one on. If someone tells me to, I am able to react; otherwise, I'm stuck in my stupor. It stinks because I'm therefore not my own boss. It is a stupid passivity that makes me rely on input from others rather than myself.

It's not fun to be so limited in this way. It stops us from communicating with others or taking responsibility for ourselves. It is confusing because I can initiate some things like eating or getting things in the house sometimes. I don't have an insight into this aspect of my illness. I just know it's there.

Autism vs. Asperger's Syndrome
February 2009

It's interesting that people see autism and Asperger's Syndrome on a continuum. I think they are completely different neurological illnesses. It's not clear that the symptoms are the same. I don't think what I have is Asperger's Syndrome in severe form. It seems like it's something else. I know kids with Asperger's Syndrome and we are really different. Their way of seeing life is different from mine. I don't really understand their highly verbal, obsessive intensity or the challenges some of them have in reading people. I'm not at all like a non-verbal version. It's not the same in the brain, I think. We need more research to explore this.

I think some forms of autism respond better to rote drills, so maybe these more verbal kids are improving more than I did in a home program. I knew a boy who mastered his flashcards drills super quickly, so obviously he had no problem pointing accurately. He also had clear speech. Lots of the girls on my ABA team worked with him too for years. I stayed around the same and he became almost normal. I was so envious, but now I suspect we had different illnesses even though we were both diagnosed with autism. I don't think it's just severity. I think it's different.

I don't think everything should be lumped under one name. I think this happens because we all have stims, poor eye contact and delays, but not every other symptom is the same. Some people talk clearly, some unclearly, some not at all. Some say things over and over. Some are depressed and some seem content with their situation. Some line things up, are rigid, and don't like change. Others cope with change. I could go on and on.

I think labels like "high" and "low functioning," and expecting us all to respond to the same treatment makes it a lot harder for people to understand how different we are. If we all have the same diagnosis, people assume it's just degree, not differences neurologically. I have noticed that there is a kind of non-verbal autism in which the intelligence is high but the person is stuck in silence like me. I see lots of kids like this. They are stuck in a kind of paralysis because the body doesn't listen to the mind's commands. If our symptoms aren't seen as different, it will not be possible to find a cure for us.

How People React to Me
February 2009

It's interesting to see who is comfortable with me and who is not. Some people have the capacity to see me as a boy, only one with challenges. Others see only strangeness. They get tense or quiet or ill at ease, then they either ignore me or talk to me as if I were two years old. It's interesting who reacts this way. I see no connection to education at all, nor age, religion, or intelligence. Some people are simply more open in their minds and hearts. It seems to me that it is a gift.

It's an interesting thing because some people we know consider themselves to be so tolerant but the whole family is obviously uncomfortable in my presence. On the other hand, we know a family that is not so impressed with their tolerance of others, they just are. I feel welcome by the whole family including the teenager. It's a test of true openness if people have the capacity to see me as a whole person with feelings and thoughts, or if I just make them uncomfortable.

I hate it when people stiffen up or stare. It is so sad because I can't tell them to stop staring, or swear at them, though I do that in my head. It's not surprising they stare if I flap my hands. Time will help me flap less, I believe, but they are rude to stare. It is a sad thing to feel so different that people need to stare. I've lived with this my whole life so I guess it shouldn't hurt me. It sometimes still does.

It's forced me to see the world in terms of those who can see me as a person with autism and those who see only autism. Even some relatives who love me struggled with this. When I was diagnosed they acted differently with me. I saw it even as a young boy. I think they were sad but they also tried to do right by treating me in terms of my autism. It was so unrelaxed. I was self-conscious of every stim. I thought they only saw my stims and my hopeless future so it was hard to see them even though I loved them.

To their credit, since I learned to write and point they see me as a boy with autism, not as an autistic boy, so people have the capacity to grow in this respect. I have seen this happen with friends of my parents and sister too. This is why we people with autism must be able to communicate our ideas so people can see us for who we are, not as we stim.

Swirling Letters
February 2009

When I was very young I taught myself to read. I loved letters and I stared at them any time I could. I would get excited and flap so my ABA team told my parents to stop letting me stare at letters. In my drills they used letters to help me label objects. I was reading then though they thought I was fixating. I didn't get to show I could read for many years. I did think, often in spelling, but not in spoken words. I visualized the word in my head. I saw the whole sentence or more. I still do, but now I am hearing the word simultaneously.

Soma didn't teach me to read. She taught me how to get my language out of my head. It was not an easy process because it was swirling internally with no way out. It's awesome to liberate my thoughts. People take this for granted and talk such dopey things all day. I choose each word carefully. I want it to matter. It's a precious gift to communicate so I treat it with care and seriousness, even if I'm joking around. It's amazing to be liberated from silence. No one should have to face this hardship. Communication is what makes us fully alive.

On Speaking Out
February 2009

I only know a small number of other kids who communicate like me. It has forced me into a trailblazer role. I'm not a brave person. I am scared of being in front of cameras or interviewers. I have decided to speak out anyway. It's not my goal to be well known. I like being anonymous, but I am determined to say what has to be said. It's not always our choice if we are brave. Sometimes it's important to do, even if you're scared.

It's my prayer that I help the world to find a better way to work with non-verbal autistic people. I have written repeatedly about how we suffer in our isolation. I saw it today with a friend of mine. He is so desperate to communicate but I observed that his feelings and his body fought him and overwhelmed him. I watched him try to communicate but he couldn't control his hand so he sat and stimmed instead. If you looked closely you could see that his eyes were full of sadness. Most people probably only saw the stimming. Then, if he goes home and is angry his parents will think he is having a fit because he is hungry or something physical. Then he will cry inside even more.

It is a story that happens every day. He is getting overwhelmed and freezes. This is one of the worst parts of autism. I know and I have been there. If my speaking out can help him to be free it will be worth conquering my fears to face people.

Empathy
February 2009

Sometimes I find it overwhelming to see my friends trapped the way they are and it seems like no one else sees. It isn't upsetting to them. They see these disabled kids who need help and are getting help. But I see kids trapped in silence who watch me use my board. I feel horrible to see them so sad, especially because I don't know if someone will ever show them the way out of their total silence. It feels like seeing prisoners in chains and I can do nothing to help. It makes me brim with feelings and act up, even though I know it's wrong. It's my job to deal with my strong emotions. It's not fair to take it out on my aide or to make disturbances in mainstream class. It's a big mistake because I make autistic people look bad and it isn't a way to help my friends and it makes things much worse.

It's puzzling to me why so many smart, insightful people miss the sorrow in my classmates' faces. Maybe you have to have experienced this pain in order to see it or to even know that this longing is there. I see it so clearly but I think many people see another cause to the mood or expression. Is it knowledge that helps me see what others don't? I think so because it is true for anything we learn. I see rocks but a geologist sees the history of the rocks. I see stars but an astronomer sees a world of celestial physics. I see grief in the faces of my friends.

Others see autistic kids in school. It's sad for me to see one of my friends in particular. He's cool and I like him. If we could talk to each other I'd be so happy because I know how much we have in common. I need a friend in school to tell things to. I like him. It's too bad he is so stuck.

I think I need to see this in a more positive light. My friends are brave and it's not always sad for them. They are loved and cared for and they also love. There is also hope for them to overcome their struggle of communication. It's interesting how I work through my feelings as I write. I feel a lot better now.

Guessing Insights
February 2009

One theory about autism is that we have no empathy. It often feels like the experts guess their insights. How do they really know? Is there a map to empathy in the brain that autistic people lack, or is it based on watching stims, or is it because Asperger's Syndrome is different than my version of autism? How do they know whether non-verbal people have empathy or not? If we lack communication, we can't tell people what we think. We can't write or gesture or show it on our faces or even control our impulses very well, so how do they know what's in our minds? They guess.

It's a problem because these guesses impact the lives of thousands of kids and their families. That is power, I tell you. I have been told that non-verbal autistic people like me, who can communicate, have a different sort of autism. The result is that these experts are unable to see that the same potential to communicate exists in many other autistic kids. This is tragic. It leaves thousands of kids stuck in boredom, isolation, and sorrow. Is this fair?

In the 1950s experts guessed that autism was a mental disorder and this was discredited. Now we are told that what I have is an empathy, learning and social disorder. Eventually, they will guess something else unless we non-verbal autistic people finally tell people the truth about our lives and experiences. I find it hard to speak, control my body or my anxiety. How else would people who can't control their body, speak, initiate, and are consumed by anxiety act than like we do? It makes sense. It's obvious if you allow yourself to see it.

Using Other People's Hands
February 2009

Many times, especially when I was small, I would grab people's hands to do things for me. The theory about this one was wrong too. Experts say it's because I see other people as objects and use their hands as a tool. How do they arrive at this brilliant conclusion? It's always amazing to me how wrong the insights have been. The experts have failed to notice that our hands are not coordinated or obeying our thoughts or that we can't verbally tell people how we need help. I mean, how else would we tell people we need help if we can't talk than by grabbing their hands? Duh. Think before you say that I can't distinguish between a person and a chair. I know the difference between a person and an object.

Visual Processing
February 2009

If I don't see something it can be hard for me to look for it. This is an awful problem because it leads my experts to conclude that I don't listen or understand directions. We went to my aunt's house yesterday. My mom asked me to hand her the flowers we brought her. My aunt was behind me. I couldn't see her. I saw my cousins and grandmother and uncle. I got embarrassed and tried to give them the flowers only to stop feeling so dumb. My behaviorists would have concluded that I didn't know the names of my relatives, so I would have had drills with their pictures on flashcards. It's so silly. Just turn my head or tell me she's standing behind me and I instantly master the drill. I have a kind of tunnel vision, I think. My behavior can be interpreted in many ways. Try looking at it the way I'm telling you and you'll see it makes the most sense.

Blank Mask
March 2009

My face is a mask that hides my true feelings. It looks flat and calm
and inside it's not. I may be laughing, or grieving, or sad, or rolling
my eyes in frustration, or interested, or excited, but my face is flat. It
is lousy, I tell you. I can't show my emotions to others. I may be angry
enough to pop but I look flappy, not mad. It's part of the lopsided
world of autism. Sometimes I feel things and I don't show it. Other
times I show too much or the wrong emotion. Sometimes if I get mad
it's overly mad or sorrow is all consuming. My body takes over and it's
like a train I can't stop, so I cry too much or get so furious it scares me
at times. I'm learning to control my emotions more. Other times my
emotions are out of whack. I laugh when I'm nervous or embarrassed
and then people think I'm disrespectful. It's a constant source of
misunderstanding. It is so frustrating. It has to be one of the most
annoying things about autism.

Initiation Disorder
March 2009

Sometimes my initiating problem is huge. I have to work on this because
initiating never comes easy to me. Many nights I am overly hot in bed
or too cold but I lie there like a dope freezing or sweating. I'll think
about how I wish someone would come and give me a blanket or
take one off me. I don't seem to be able to react to my needs of the
moment. It is weird because I do react to my desire for food. There I
initiate too much. I love to eat, so maybe that's why.

For example, one time I was walking with my mom and she slipped
and fell on her knee. I saw it and I saw she was hurt but just like with
my inability to respond to my temperature in bed, I was stuck. I felt
terrible because I really wanted to help her and ask if she was okay.
Instead I stood there like a statue. Luckily she was able to get up and
walk home. If not, it would have been a disaster. Now I see how I am
too helpless because of this deficit. It's necessary that I learn to react

to my needs more and to be able to help if others need help. How I will do this I have no concept, but I have to figure out something.

My Body Has a Mind of Its Own
March 2009

My body is wired in some peculiar way. It is like a faulty connection. Sometimes it is listening to me well, yet it is still not reliable. Other times it is a struggle to get it to do what I want, not just in terms of coordination but sometimes simply doing what it should. It drives me nuts. It's hard to describe what I mean. It's not obeying me in sports. It's slow and takes too long to react. If I miss a catch it takes me too long to get the ball. It is not listening to my head. It stands with no reaction in games when it should run. It stands if I want to bounce a ball or dribble. I drop the ball and stand too long until it rolls away. It is idiotic because it makes me flap my hands.

It is so strange that I can't do what I want in this way. I have learned to ride a two-wheel bike, scooter, and I swim. I'm strong in many ways, but strength doesn't get my body to obey my brain. It's a paradox because even if it listens, it doesn't mean that it can respond. For example, today my mom asked me to open my window while we were waiting in the parked car. It seems ridiculous to say that I know what a window is, but my hand acted on its own repeatedly. I kept opening the car door instead. It was scary because I was forced to repeat this error. I mean that my mind knew window and my hand insisted on the door. It's worse than that though because then people deduce that I don't know the difference between a window and a door.

It was a rough day in that way. Later my mom asked me to hand her a bag. I kept handing her a piece of paper the bag was near. It's another horrible feature of autism, especially because it makes people sure we don't understand language. It happens less often now but it was common when I was small in my ABA drills. I wanted to touch a card but my hand had another plan so I had to redo drills until my hand got it. Not my head. It knew everything. My hand had to learn the drill. It's something for the neurologists to study. This is why so many parents think their kids don't understand them.

I really don't understand why my body can listen to my thoughts some of the time and other times my body refuses to listen. This causes real problems for me especially if I have been told to do some task. Most of the time I win and my body does the right thing, but when it goes wrong, it's like it's not me but like an invader is manipulating my body at those moments. I know it sounds nutty and it is a strange thing, almost like a tic or a compulsion that is physical and against my wishes. It leads to frustration for me because it scares me. I have a fear that it is winning. Intellectually I know I am getting stronger but I can't shake the fear. I am striving to have my body obey me more. I need this to recover, for sure.

I Wish I Could Talk
March 2009

If I could talk it would be the greatest thing imaginable. Even though I can express my thoughts in pointing, it's an inferior option to verbal communication. I lag behind. I don't always have a letter board nearby. I am stuck in silence often. It is lonely because I think of things to say on the inside but outside I'm still quiet. I'm grateful to have my letter board but I want so badly to speak. I really don't know why my brain doesn't connect to my mouth. It's like the synapses stop in the middle, or something. The road to speech follows a path my brain loses, so I make sounds or I say the wrong thing, or I say nothing at all. It's awful to live in such silence. I am funny and fun and no one my age knows it because I can't keep up in conversation or play. I wish I could overcome this sooner so that I could be having fun with friends too.

Test Validity
March 2009

For years I have had tests that proved how dumb I am. At least that's what it felt like. It is awful to be smart and to know that the School District sees you as mentally retarded because you can't show what you know. In my case my mom finally had me tested privately in a way I could actually answer on my letter board. That was the first time I was given a way to communicate my knowledge during a test. I was ten and it showed that my vocabulary was at least a twelfth grade level even though in school we were still looking at toddler books. My math, which was so delayed in school they thought I couldn't count to three, was grade level. It actually was higher but I didn't cooperate enough to be tested more. Thanks to this I got out of my rudimentary education in autism class.

Imagine the results if I tested the teachers in academic knowledge but denied them speech, or writing, or letter boards, and they couldn't gesture. If they did poorly I could insist, the way people did with me, that it's because they are cognitively low. Obviously if you take away communication people can't show what they know.

Mixed Senses
March 2009

It's interesting that my perception of the world is different than typical people. It's like my senses mix together. I see qualities in people like color. I don't mean race. I mean a quality or glow that rises off them. It's like a hint of their soul, in a way. It's lovely to see. It helps me to sense who is open and ready to accept me. I feel best about blue or purple glows. These tend to be intuitive people. Colors can shift too. My mom is blue but she can be red if she is angry. Soma is more purple. She is super blue. Many of my experts have been brown or yellow or red. I can't explain it but I've always seen it.

I also taste objects. To me they seem incomplete without a taste. Their taste is as obvious to me as their appearance. I think this is one reason I still mouth objects so frequently. If I don't mouth the object I either feel annoyed or it's like I missed part of it. I know this seems odd but it's just one more interesting attribute of my disease.

If I hear notes in music I see each note visually. This is called synesthesia. Each one is as visually distinct as it is auditorally. Bach is geometric. Beethoven is like very long leaps of fire and light. Prokofiev is intricate scenes of lights and movement. Mozart is curly bands of lights and rosy colors. Jazz is sharp angles of light. Opera is lots of really huge deep lightning bolts. Pop is short simple bands of light. Rap is not a pretty sight. It is like an angry visual mess. I don't enjoy it, but I do like samba and Latin rhythms. Those have cool bouncy lights and colors.

If I hear some music I get hot or cold. It's like a full sensory experience of sound, sight and temperature. It's almost like a show in 3-D. It's totally absorbing, but it's not my choice. I see it whether I like to or not. I get uncomfortable by lots of big vocal music like opera or R & B singing. Those feel like too much pressure. Then I'm bombarded by lots of dramatic and over-stimulating visual images. It's not at all enjoyable. That's why I usually don't like vocal music.

It's interesting to experience things on more than one sensory level. It can be a total experience in both good and bad ways. To see music takes music to another level, however it is also possible for me to get overwhelmed because my senses bombard me with so much information. It's like anything, if you get too much of a good thing it's bad.

One Way to Prove I am Really Communicating
March 2009

Last year when I was in the fifth grade, I finally got out of my remedial level class. They put me in a class of verbal autistic kids with academic instruction that I'd never had before, mainstreaming, and I had to sit long periods of time. My teacher was nice, but new and inexperienced. She never had a kid like me before. No one thought I was smart or even deserved to be there. It was difficult or worse. My foolish reaction was to swear at my aide. She knew I was smart and tried to defend me. I was so isolated inside and mad and I took it out on her. That was unfair because she was nice to me. I swore often and then the school saw I was really communicating. That's irony. All I had to do was point to "F-U," and they said, "Oh, he is a lot smarter than we gave him credit for." It was a bad year tasting anger all time. I am feeling good now so I don't repeat these errors.

Talking is Really Hard
March 2009

I saw my old speech teacher today at a celebration for another autistic boy. I saw how much she cares and wants the best for me. It was nice to see her and catch up. It amazed me how different it was to see her because now I can communicate and tell her my thoughts when before I was stuck in silence, and that stank. In the past she told me often that I didn't try, and basically told me that I didn't speak because I was lazy. I was so resentful of her because she didn't understand that for me talking is hard. So, so, so, so, so, so, so, so, so, so, hard. It's like talking in an underwater world with no tongue. In other words, so, so, so, so, so, so, so, so, so, hard.

Since we autistic kids all want to talk and we can't, it should be obvious that it's not lazy kids, lazy parents, or something else. IT'S HARD! That's why the letter board is a lifesaver. In the years it takes me to speak I can express my thoughts and ideas, get a regular education, and be a member of a group, or a part of a conversation. I still want to talk verbally more than anything, but I can't sit in silence until then.

I know all the people I used to work with thought they were doing the right thing, and maybe it was the right thing for some kids, though not for me. If each could accept me and believe in me now I'd be so happy. My old speech teacher accepted me and today saw with her own eyes that I write and use a big vocabulary and am smart and that speech is great but it's too hard to access for conversations. I'm sure it is a marvelous thing for her to talk to a formerly "locked-in-silence" kid. It was nice for me to have the opportunity to talk to her out of my silent jail. If I could, I'd open the locks for all my friends and other autistic kids.

Piano
March 2009

Piano is helping me to use my brain differently. It is so hard right now to do different things with each hand. I can't seem to get both hands to listen. It's frustrating to be so clumsy. I know it's a skill I must practice. I will and I'll get it. Still, it's very hard now. My teacher thinks it will help the two sides of my brain to communicate better. I know it's possible to heal some brain injuries. My grandmother fell and had a terrible injury in her brain. She was totally messed up. She couldn't talk, eat by herself or walk. She recovered and is fine now. If we knew where my illness was in my brain we could combat it more effectively. In the meantime, I'll have to keep practicing piano and exercising my body. It's good to do both in any case even if I wasn't autistic.

Trust, Aura and Communication
March 2009

I know people wonder why I am selective with whom I use my letter board. It leads some to doubt because people think I should use my board with everyone. I wrote about anxiety and autism but it is obvious that trust is an issue in communication. It's like this: I point if I'm relaxed with someone or if I absolutely need to communicate. I made myself learn to communicate with my aides in school and my tutor because I have to get an education. It's always been a road to motivating me if I'm learning, but the process of trusting is slow. It's weird because I can love someone and enjoy their company and know they believe in me and still resist pointing with them. It's partly because some people are so impatient or seem to test me or talk to me in such a patronizing way, even if unintentional, and sometimes it's due to my own anxiety. Either way I stop trying. Then the other person gets frustrated and it's worse.

Not only that, it helps if I see a blue glow. I don't mean to hurt anyone's feeling but some people I love are brown, red and yellow. This is hard to explain. My mom is blue and my dad is yellow. He is the greatest dad I could imagine but when I see yellow I get tense when we point. I wish I could overcome this because I'm dying to joke with him. I can do math equations with him, no problem, so I'm starting to get over my issue. I don't see why it matters what color the glow is because I trust my dad, so I need to see yellow as a sunray not a stopping ray.

My aide is green. That's not blue or yellow. My old aide was yellow. I even overcame that because I needed to communicate so badly in school. My point is that the glow affects me emotionally. It is like another sense causing me to be selective with the people I point with, but intellectually I know that it's not really accurate because some great people are yellow or other colors. It's my intention to find a way to point with all people, though I may never relax if someone tells me "touch your nose." That is a very brown glow, I'm telling you.

Autism and Relationships
March 2009

People think that disabled people have no interest in romance. It's wrong. I think about girls just like any other twelve year old boy, but I'm not ready to find a girlfriend. I know I need to work on my illness long before I'm someone a girl would like to be with. It doesn't matter if I'm cute or not if I flap my hands.

I'm not even trying to meet girls now because I'm too shy. I get nervous in social situations. I need to learn to relax more with new people. I hope I can overcome this because I'd like to get a girlfriend when I'm older. I have the same desires in life as anyone but a harder mountain to climb to get there. It's true for anyone with life-changing circumstances. I know I have to be a lot better, more appropriate in my behavior, calmer and more outgoing to have a girl interested in me. It's not in my ability yet but with hard work I hope it will be. Normal kids are sure lucky in this respect.

Why a Little Arm Support Helps
March 2009

It helps many autistic people to have someone touch or even support their arm when writing or communicating. This is due to our trouble initiating and getting our bodies to obey our minds. This slight touch seems to help unlock the sort of paralysis I have described. No one needs to support me, thanks to Soma's instruction. This is important because then people see I'm independently moving my hand. Then it's hard to claim it's not me.

Some kids I know need the touch support to write or point. To some, they will always be seen as puppets of their facilitator even though the support is so minimal. I heard that in the past some stupid people did manipulate the writing of some kids. The result is that all support is therefore suspect. That is unreasonable. In a disorder of anxiety, initiation, and a body that doesn't obey the mind, a little support is a lifesaver. When I play the piano or do some other tasks with fine motor I get a slight touch of support on my arm, but no one doubts it's me doing it. It's different with communication. A little wrist support and you are a zombie being manipulated by a control freak parent. That theory manages to insult both kid and parent.

When I was small my mom had a hunch I understood everything. It was when ABA dominated my life and home. I loved *The Jungle Book* and I had a picture book with the Disney story. One day I sat with my mom and she lightly supported my arm. She asked me to find characters. I did it all perfectly. She got excited and told my dad that I understood everything. He said, "Are you sure you weren't inadvertently moving his arm?" I remember this conversation well because it so upset me. She would know if she moved me, I'd think.

It's not his fault. It was the theories he'd been taught to believe that any support was manipulated, even accidentally. He told her to try again with no support. Of course I got it all wrong. This was proof that I didn't really know the characters of my favorite movie. It was so lousy because my mom didn't persist in trying. She didn't trust her own instincts. How could I tell her she was right? I died inside a little because I came close to freedom and ABA won. If you saw my heart, it was torn into pieces. It took years to find a way to show my mom again what I knew. This time she didn't give up though no one believed her. Thanks to this I have a healing heart.

Shut Out of the Discussion
March 2009

My therapist was invited to present a speech at an autism conference. She asked me and my parents if she could present on me. She filmed me communicating each time I saw her. She thought I had a lot to teach people. I was nervous about it but I also welcomed the opportunity to educate professionals in the autism field about my experiences with autism and my educational challenges. Yesterday she told my mom that her presentation proposal was rejected because I use a letter board that someone holds. My therapist told them that I point independently and that no one touches me when I point. The people who run the conference told her that my method of communication is not accepted. I guess someone holding a piece of paper in front of me with letters on it is really invasive, so I can sure understand why they wouldn't want my story to be told.

It's not too surprising. Some people prefer not to see the truth. If I'm doing what I do it means others can too. If they refuse to see it, they don't have to change how they teach kids. I laugh because they assume I'm a fraud and they've never seen me, met me, or even seen a film of me. I guess that watching the films and asking my therapist questions would be too risky. Someone might get convinced that a retarded autistic kid was really intact in thinking. That would mean that that they would need to see autism in a new way. Can't let that happen. Suppressing alternative viewpoints is better.

It happened to me another time when a speech I wrote for a dinner banquet was printed in a magazine. The program director got a call from an autism expert. "Be careful that it's true and that he really wrote that. I've never seen this kind of advanced language skills in twenty-five years of working with autistic children. If he really wrote that, he would be one in a million." I felt so mad when the director told me this. I told him that she was blinded by her professional biases. He told me that he told her that he guessed I was one in a million then.

Am I so threatening that they would rather believe I'm a fraud or a well rehearsed dummy rather than be what I am? If I had a stroke would I become retarded? I couldn't talk or move the way I want. What if I were deaf or had cerebral palsy? Would that mean I can't think? If I could talk I'd be smart but because I point and type I'm not? Because someone holds my letter board I'm not pointing myself but I am if I'm at the table with my computer? If you refuse to believe in me does it mean I'm a fraud, or that experts are not open-minded?

Why not let her present? They can argue or disagree and see me for themselves. By not letting me be seen they reveal that my message needs to be heard and I will pursue channels other than professional experts to tell my story. I'm laughing because I realized that I've always been scared of my experts but in some ways my existence scares them too.

Sign Language
March 2009

Many people ask me why I don't communicate in sign language. They think because I'm limited verbally that sign language is the logical communication for me. It's not for many reasons. First, I hear. I'm oriented to speech and talking, not visual language. I also have fine motor delays so the hand shapes in sign language are really difficult for me.

My mom knows sign language. She taught me some but it was for fun, not to be my way of communicating. She told me that sign language uses facial expression and my face is often blank. It has a different grammar and I use English and think in English, not in signs. I use a large vocabulary. My mom told me that in sign language there are fewer word choices. For example there is one sign for "big" and you use facial expressions and larger or smaller arm movements for emphasis. If I type or point on a letter board I can be more specific.

I can spell large, huge, gigantic, enormous and so on.

Pointing and typing work well for me because I don't need precise fine motor hand shapes. Some people think I should stop pointing and switch to sign language. Even a neurologist I saw at first suggested it for me. It would end my ability to express myself for all the reasons I've listed. Inside I am thinking in English words and I use these same words on my letter board or keyboard.

Proprioception
March 2009

If I have my eyes closed I don't know where my hands are. I understand now that it's a sense called proprioception that lets us know where our bodies are in space. My proprioception is messed up. I need my eyes to tell me where my hands and legs are. This is hard because it means I have to visually pay attention to my body. It interferes with many physical sports especially if I can't see my legs. It is not nice at night because I can't tell what position I am in, in bed in the dark. I tend to use my blankets to give me pressure by wrapping them around me so I can feel where my body is. It helps enormously. I always do it, even on hot days, because I have to know where my body is. My exercising is helping me to feel it more. My body is beginning to connect more to my brain. I'm determined to overcome this challenge.

Today in piano I used my right and left hand together. In the recent past this would have been impossible. I am also more able to do exercises involving coordination than ever before. I want to get fit. I believe it will help me to live more fully. My body has been my master all my life. I'd like to turn it around.

Liberated by Assistive Technology
March 2009

I'm hoping to get a better assistive communication device. I'm excited to have the opportunity to test one and to try others. I think it will be great, kind of like having the ability to talk. Instead of having someone read my words, I type and push a button and the machine speaks my words. That is almost like my own voice. I know it isn't perfect but it's much better than what I've had up until now. It is freedom.

Yesterday with a device I borrowed I talked on the phone. It was so liberating. Not just, "How are you?" but a real conversation. I joked. They laughed. They asked me questions. I answered. Like you do. Only it was my first time. It's so meaningful to me to have my own voice speaking my thoughts to others. I'm almost thirteen so I'd say it's about time.

"Theory of Mind" When it Matters
March 2009

It is frustrating when smart people misunderstand me. I guess it's because I hope they will see me the right way. I really see myself as normal internally but blocked in mind/body connection, so I do things I don't want to do like flap or grab things I shouldn't. I can't do things I want to do like talk, dance, play basketball, or write neatly. I can't stop my emotions from pouring out of my body in flapping, glares, or tensing up, but I *can* understand my predicament. I look odd. I have poor eye contact. I remove myself from people if I'm nervous. I stim. I seem to be unsympathetic to others because I don't hug or move from my sofa to share the space unless told to. I don't initiate well, but it doesn't mean I don't have empathy. I care about other people. I love people. I worry about people. I need people to care about me. Just like anyone else.

Yesterday a professional I work with suggested that the reason I didn't feel sorry for my sister when she had a problem involving soccer is because, as an autistic person, I lacked "theory of mind," or empathy into the point of view of someone else. After knowing me as well as she does, I was surprised that she interpreted my behavior through the prism of autism theories, rather than just seeing me. I know my sister was bummed and disappointed at first, but she recovered quickly and is doing well in sports. My reaction is not due to a lack of empathy. It just didn't seem like a catastrophe to me. She suggested that even if it wasn't, I should have empathy for her suffering. This may be true. On the other hand, I have had thousands of small rejections and losses in my life at about the same magnitude as her situation. Every day I just have to deal with these upsetting things with little empathy from people. Still, I try to be thoughtful when I can be. I can't phone people or initiate a group hug, but if I have access to a letter board or keyboard I ask how they are. Both of my parents point out that I am thoughtful in this respect.

I'm sure people who are dealing with big issues understand what I'm talking about. It is possible I can try to be more understanding of small losses, but it's not a one way street. My feelings are often hurt when people ignore me, or stiffen near me, or move away. I know I'm weird so I take responsibility and I'll work on it, but do all these people also lack theory of mind because they make no attempt to identify with *my* circumstances? I beg people to understand that just because I don't show a lot of emotion doesn't mean I don't care.

It is possible that other forms of autism have more impairment in the area of "theory of mind." If these people are verbal it is easy to assume that non-verbal autistic people are the same. How can we show otherwise when we are so locked in?

Autism is a Deep Pit
April 2009

I saw an autistic boy today who was so locked in his inner world. It is hard to see and to remember that. His helper tried hard to engage him but he was lost in his sensory world and tuned her out. She tried to help and he resisted her. Yet I think he is smart.

Autism is like a deep pit filled with sand that is blocking your way out. You see that people are trying to help but it is not easy to move in the sand. If you try, you may reverse the sand and sink deeper. If you do nothing, you are sad inside. If you disappear in your senses you escape the rotten frustration so it's like a drug. It's a high in a way of lights and colors. Then it's even harder to reach the autistic kid because he is in a pit, in sand that sinks, and he is watching a laser light show in his head. It's lonely in the pit, even with loving people nearby. This boy was impossible to connect to and I see how frustrating it is for families in this situation. He is like a ghost because he is there, but not there. Yet he is internally there, hearing, seeing and feeling, even though he is so remote. It's a long path to connecting to others. He has a long journey because he is lost in his own world. Stims dominate his life so he is not relating to people well.

What to do for him? He needs communication, I'm sure, not just counting numbers or repeating words which is what they kept trying to do with him. He needs to get out and do things that engage his mind and body. He needs rules. He was invasive and bratty. It reminds me to work more on this too. He isn't lost if he is shown how to climb out of the pit to a life that is external too because there are people who love him who want to know the boy inside, and not just the behaviors outside.

Body Awareness through Exercise
April 2009

Many autistic people love swimming. I can stay in a pool for hours until I'm a prune. I can go into a freezing pool or ocean. I get cold but I need to be in the water. It's so compelling I must do it. It's because in the water I can feel my whole body. In the water I feel my legs and my core and my arms. It's good to be in the water because it applies gentle pressure to my body. Outside of the water I need to look to see my legs' positions. On dry land I feel like my body is unreal or not even part of me sometimes. This is starting to get better thanks to my exercising. My body is listening more and becoming more coordinated. I can do things now I never could before like bilateral movements and balancing on an exercise ball for sit-ups. If my body wakes up I'll be on my way to getting better.

It's important to get fit too. My family is active and athletic. It stank when I alone was out of shape. I'm happy that I too can be in better shape. When my mom first began working out with me I resisted because it was so hard, but she toughed it out and hired a great trainer for me too. He is thinking about how to wake up my muscles. Now I enjoy exercising. Hard to believe because I never did before. I'm hoping to connect my no-good body, as I always thought of it, to my mind. My body isn't bad. It's just disconnected. Exercise, I believe, builds my neural connections. I used to scratch my legs because I hated my body so much. Not anymore. My legs are running, hiking, bike riding, riding scooters, just fine. It's like anyone. It's a long process to get into good condition but I think even an autistic person can.

Sad Families
April 2009

It's not just autistic kids who get depressed. Their parents do too. I see it often. The parents look so grief-stricken or exhausted. Some seem like they've given up on their kids. It's easy to see why. The kids are so limited and don't respond to rules so parents start to go nuts. It's awful because often the kid is just not in control of his impulses or his body. For example, I saw a kid who couldn't sit still at a dinner banquet. To me he seemed nervous and overwhelmed. To his dad he was embarrassing and disruptive. The dad seemed furious and really sad too. He looked so tired and even despairing in between losing his temper. The son wasn't malicious. He was not being bad. He is suffering double because he can't overcome his sensory overwhelming world, his body and his sorrow, and then he is misunderstood by those he loves most. His dad loves him. I could see that. He also resented the burden of his son. Maybe if he understood what his son was going through better it would help to mend their relationship. It hurt to see them both suffer so much.

My Start with the Rapid Prompting Method (RPM)
April 2009

The first time I communicated beyond my immediate needs was with my mom at age seven. She asked me why I didn't show her before that I could write. I told her that I didn't know how to. Autistic people don't have the means to climb out of their pit on their own. Teach us to do it and we won't seem dumb. It's Soma's genius that she found a way to teach us to communicate. It's amazing to me that despite her accomplishments she still has to fight the doubt of experts daily. A lot of people don't recognize her methods. Research it and see it for yourself. I mean, stop attacking things you know nothing about!

Soma taught me to strive for real communication. At first it was hard and I was aggressive and pinched her. It wasn't just me. Her arms had many pinch marks on them. That didn't faze her. She kept on insisting I learn. No reinforcers or tickles or "good jobs" or "no's." She taught me science on my first visit. It was odd because it was advanced. No one did that before. It was nice that she knew I was smart. In school I was retarded. In Soma's office I was gifted. She was tough and didn't let me get away with anything. This helped me work and try.

I remember the first independent sentence I pointed with Soma was "Touch my nose." I guess I thought that educators wanted me to do that. She said, "No, no, no. We don't do that here." Freedom! She knew immediately what I meant. She taught me to sit and learn for forty-five minutes with no break, no tickles, no food. It was like a miracle after my years of drills and silence. Of course when my school teacher and my ABA supervisor observed me in my early days there, they looked for prompts. Soma doesn't deny prompts. Duh! Her method is called Rapid **Prompting**. If she called it "Slow Flashcards" it would be okay? I was tasting my first real communication and all my experts saw were the prompts, not the communication.

I was a beginner. I wonder how they could fail to get that? I mean, it's a skill. It takes time. It amazed me that they saw prompts but missed my communicating. Is it ABA's contention that their prompts are okay but Soma's are not? They often prompted me in my flashcard sessions.

My ABA notes indicated if I needed a prompt or if I had mastered a drill. Couldn't they understand that I needed prompts with Soma then, but now have mastered it?

It seems to me that so many are truly blinded by their professional biases. My dad has a joke about a doctoral student in physics he knew. He was describing his research and he said, "The data that didn't fit the model we threw away." The scientists were shocked because if the data doesn't fit the model you adjust the model to fit the data, you don't pretend the data doesn't exist, but in that case it was just his poor English. I think my experts threw away Soma's data because it challenged their model. If I am harsh on them, I think I have a right. My ABA supervisor told my mom that it made no difference if I could communicate or not. I would continue to be taught in the same way with the same flashcards and drills as if I still didn't know my verbs, categories, adjectives, pronouns and so on. That's when my mom and dad decided to stop ABA. She told me that the whole team sat and argued with her that I couldn't really communicate because I didn't with them.

How could I with them? I only got drills or behavior modification. How was I to communicate with them? Spontaneously erupt in song and dance? Talking was impossible. Writing I could do with support but they denied me that. RPM they thought was a quack science. So, what's left? The data that didn't fit the model they threw away. If I was silent there, I must be silent everywhere, including internally.

I always credit Soma with saving me. She helped me to communicate and move past my resentment. This ultimately freed me to grow as a person. I have my heroes; my mom and dad, Soma, and several others who see me as I am and help me to move on in life. Every day I realize how lucky I am to have been liberated from silence and to be welcomed by so many as a friend and equal. My struggles are not over but I can lead my experts to help me now.

Remembering I have Two Sides
April 2009

I have a habit of washing one hand. I often forget about my right hand and need to be reminded to wash it. My dad suggests it may reflect a lack of connectivity between the two sides of my brain. It's one more clue to unlock autism.

Short, Long and Photographic Memory
April 2009

My short term memory is lousy. I am easily distracted from my goal. Maybe that's not memory. Maybe it's attention. I know it is a big problem. It bothers me a lot. It always makes people mad at me. I am kind of lost in my head if I'm distracted. For example, if I am getting dressed sometimes I am fine and finish in a few minutes independently. Other times I am really spacey. I pace or flap or stare in space. I get one sock on, or only my pants, then I am in a sort of trance, pacing, half done with my task. Where do I go? I have no idea. It's like, I'm here. I'm not. It's bad because I need prompts to get things done often. If someone tells me "Finish!" I'm like, "Huh?" It's like I'm emptied of thought. I need to be reminded of what I was doing.

It's not pleasant. I feel like it's a seizure or something but I was tested when I was small and they said I didn't have seizures. On the other hand, I remember some things forever. I can see whole pages of books in my head. I can get distracted by my memories. It's sort of one more autism paradox. I never forget from ten years ago but I can't remember to finish getting dressed. It's one more thing that makes people think I am dumb when I am not.

I am able to remember details in books, conversations, and other things too well. It is a terrible thing because it fills my head up with things it doesn't need, but if I need to say a word I can't recall it, or at least my mouth can't. No assumptions about intelligence help. It's like the conduit is broken. It's as if my knowledge is interrupted on the way to my mouth. That is autism's downside.

We think. We understand. We know. We have to sit and flap and make gibberish and then we are seen as retarded. Maybe there are some retarded autistic people, but not as many as you think. We fail intelligence tests because we are suffering from an output disorder. We are in there, but so blocked, and only a few of us have been shown the way out.

My thoughts get lost on the way to my mouth but thank God they don't get lost in my pointing. I don't know why this is but it just is. The mind is a world that we don't understand yet. We have much to learn about so many aspects of the brain. No one understands autism neurologically yet which is why no treatment should be seen as the gospel. I know I am rambling from memory to communication to treatment but they are interrelated. I remembered all my drills. I couldn't communicate my ideas unless I practiced over and over until it was automatic, but my treatment continued to be based on the idea that I didn't remember or understand. If I drilled my instructors in another language they couldn't speak, but understood, and I counted their errors as proof of lack of knowledge year after year, you'd have my childhood. A maze without end. My output disorder confirmed my ignorance to them so I kept turning in the maze to another dead-end. Typing is the way out of my maze and may be for other autistic people as well.

I know parents strive to do the best for their kids. I don't mean to make stressed, worried parents even more tired. It's hard to be the person with autism and hard to be the parent. In autism education, teachers and parents make decisions for the autistic kid based on external performance only. How else if the kid is non-verbal or has limited speech? Since so few of us are taught to communicate, many educators and parents never hear the autistic kid's point of view.

Soma changed my future from stims and drills to one in which I can imagine college and even more. I may never talk well verbally but I have a computer. Technology will improve so that the voice will get more natural in time and word prediction will get better. I can continue to work on self control and my impulses and my body, and I will improve. I am hopeful when once I was hopeless. I want to give this hope to more autistic people too. I am sure it is worth it otherwise I wouldn't be writing this book in the knowledge that I will no longer be private when I'm so shy, and that I may be unfairly judged by biased people. I believe autistic people, even twelve year old autistic people, need to contribute to the discussion about autism education and treatment.

My School Education
April 2009

One aspect of Soma's theory is to speed up education in order to stop our stims or anxiety from intruding. This rapid approach helped me to learn to focus. Slow approaches make me distracted. School is often slow and special education slower still. In a slow class I'll enter my stims because I hate sitting and waiting. I bore easily and I learn fast. It may be hard for me to sit quietly in class but I am learning and thinking. In a slow academic environment I really stop paying attention. That's what happened last year. My teacher taught slowly for slow learners. My mind races. I get it fast. Then I wait for them to get it too. This is where my impulse control is a problem because I can't just sit in silence so I get disruptive. Of course, then people may decide I need an even slower class. It's a trying situation because I need an advanced education but my behavior is not as developed as my intellect.

My education has been a strange one. I taught myself to read when I was very young, but no one knew. I got "educated" in flashcards of simple infant concepts forty hours a week in my home program starting before I was three. Then when I went to school I did simple activities and games but no academics. I saw the same ABC tape for three years because we supposedly didn't know our letters, and math was even worse. It assumed I couldn't even count when I already multiplied and divided. My teacher told my mom that I might do multiplication at home because some autistic people can, but that didn't mean I understood what a number was.

In fourth grade I saw a tutor at home who taught me essay styles, social studies, math and grade level work. This saved me. My teacher was teaching me nothing at school. I was losing my patience with my experts who concluded that it was too stressful to challenge us with interesting lessons, so I sort of stopped caring altogether. My parents taught me interesting things at home like science and literature, but in school it was like pre-school, and it stank.

This went on until fifth grade. Then I was sent to a so-called "high functioning" autism class where all the students talked and had body control but they did grade level work at a slower pace. It was a taste of academics but I didn't fit in because I learned so differently from my classmates. I'm sad to say my behavior was awful. I'm embarrassed now to think of it but I was totally stressed out in my suddenly academic environment. I alone was non-verbal. No one thought I deserved to be there. I had to ride the bus for an hour and a half each way because the school was very rigid and wouldn't let me be dropped off ten minutes late by a much shorter ride.

Now in Middle School I am mainstreamed in math and science. My classes are huge and I struggle to sit and to be quiet, but the kids accept me and my teacher is terrific. Then I go to an autism class with so-called "low functioning" autistic kids, who I am sure are cognitively fast, but who can't control their bodies or communicate their thoughts. The teacher is nice and energetic but I am the only one who gets grade level instruction in my other subjects. It's lonely because no matter where I am, I am the only one who points or types.

In elementary school I really cared about my teacher who I had for three years. She was loving and warm and thought I was smart. I coped because I loved her, but that's not enough to compensate for a lack of interesting lessons. It was even worse after I finished her class when I still had no interesting lessons but my teacher wasn't someone I felt a connection to. Then it was like a really bad movie you have to see a million times. Now it's a lot better. I am more interested in school than ever before. I hope that it continues to move in a positive direction.

Age 13, Starting to Let Go of the Past

As you read, when I was twelve I still had the resentments of many years of silent frustration brewing in me. Internally I was struggling to move on emotionally, and to feel happier, but I needed to deal with my early misery when my autism stopped me from being educated at the level I needed. As I started seeing success in my daily life and came to analyze my autism more, I began to feel more and more hopeful and this allowed me to begin to let go of my anger.

Inspiration
May 2009

Recently I have been watching some re-broadcasts of the 2008 Paralympics in China. It inspires me. These athletes are fit, fast and tough. Some have no feet, arms, or are deformed in some way. Many have been in accidents that changed their lives completely. No self pity. Maybe sadness, of course, but no self pity. They say, "OK. I lost my leg. What can I do with one? I am an athlete with one leg."

I saw one sprinter, Jim Bob Bizzell, who had lost his leg about a year and a half earlier. Wow. He ran so fast, and proudly, and he was triumphant even though he came in second. He was defeated by a sprinter, Oscar Pistorius, with no legs. Fast fast fast. I watched it and I thought about how many years I've spent in self pity. My body is a problem for me. It doesn't obey my mind well most of the time and I've hated it because of that. Many times I gave up because it was so hard to get my body to listen to me and I doubted it ever would.

I have been working on my body and it is possible to get more control. I will have to work harder at it just like these athletes. I saw swimmers with one arm, or one leg, or no arms, and I knew it was not easy for them to get where they were. How easy to be on the sofa and watch TV in self-pity. How hard to say, "I won't be defeated by my challenges." Why not me? I can work on my body too. I can run, or swim, or skateboard if I try, but I need to practice more than average. Oscar Pistorius said, "You're not disabled by the disabilities you have. You are able by the abilities you have." Yes! By focusing on my abilities I can grow them. By focusing on my disabilities I am stuck.

I want to add one important thing. The tendency in autism education has been to focus on our disabilities and deficits. I can't do certain things with my body no matter how much I try. I doubt I'll ever be able to sing, for example. Even conversing verbally may be out of reach, but I can do other things instead. I can think, point on a letter board or type. I can improve these skills, my abilities, and become more independent. If the only focus is on my speech I stay stuck because it's a disability, not an ability. It's like asking the wheelchair athletes to stand and run. It's not available to them, but by building up their arms they enhance what works. It's easier to see this when it concerns a physical disability but harder with autism because it's a neurological problem. I am determined to fight this because it's time to expand my abilities and let my disabilities live in peace.

Sensitive Senses
May 2009

I get so miserable in the heat. It's like I'm roasting in an oven. It is so overwhelming to try to cope with P.E., or to walk in the heat on these scorching days. I don't know if this is part of autism. One mom told me she thinks so. I did notice that my classmates suffered in the heat more than average. Our sensory system is so over reactive I wouldn't be surprised if my heat regulation was too sensitive. I hear too much. I see too much. I guess I overheat too much too.

My senses are strong. I can hear through walls and across rooms. I have to struggle to filter out the multitude of sounds I hear. You intuitively know what sound is important. This is lucky because I can't. The air conditioner, the dog bark, the conversation, the fridge hum are all equal in my mind. When I was little it was too much information. It overwhelmed so much I would tune out and stim. I have learned to concentrate on speech, but if there are two or more conversations at the same time I am struggling to keep on one and it's hard. For example, in a restaurant or a dinner party the hum of the voices is like a loud horrible Babel to me. It's at best a trying situation. At worst, it's a punishment.

Visually too I get overwhelmed. It's as if I see everything foreground and nothing in the background. Sometimes I see in a tunnel and I miss the sides. Other times I see the sides and miss the big picture because I'm lost in details. It stinks because it increases my incorrect responses often. I am much improved in this but many times I fetched the wrong item because I didn't see it was right in front of me. It's another clue into autism for neurologists to look into.

Fleeting Windows
May 2009

Have you ever wondered what an autistic child feels inside? After all, he can't say how he feels verbally or write it. Often his face is like a mask or inappropriate for the situation, but if you look closely, carefully, quickly you will see the real feeling behind the mask. It may last no more than a second or two, but it appears, even if briefly. It's like a window that opens and shuts in an instant. I think most people miss it because it happens so fast and it's imbedded in masks or stims. I bet if you filmed an autistic person in slow motion you would be able to catch these glimpses. I see these expressions clearly now. So does my mom. It is a look of sorrow or gratitude or laughter or eye rolling on the inside. I see relief if my mom or I show recognition of someone's emotional state or intelligence. I see annoyance if someone is treated like a baby long after he is not one. I see sorrow in someone's eyes if he is stuck or can't communicate his thoughts. I see hope in their eyes when they see how I can communicate.

So often we non-verbal folks are misunderstood but we sometimes reveal our true feelings in these windows. Too bad they are so short because they are hard to see, but they are there. Why it fleets so fast I don't know. I sense they are covered by stims or by autism's paralyzing effects and so they are buried. Maybe with practice we can learn to show our true feelings more.

Phobias
May 2009

Most autistic people have phobias. I know so many kids who are terrified of my dogs. We have three. All are nice and social, but the kids are terrified and scream as if the dogs were aggressive. I used to have a phobia of small showers. My senses got overwhelmed in them, like an intense claustrophobia. My mom and dad made me learn to deal with it, and now I'm fine. I was also afraid of horses, and theaters in the dark, and the rides at amusement parks. I wanted to ride them but I felt so panicked I couldn't get on. It's a lot like a panic attack, I think. It's improving now that I feel more in charge of my life but there's still a lot of things I can't get myself to do.

Games, Pretend and Theory of Mind
May 2009

I'm not into games. It's lost on me why Sorry or cards or checkers or Monopoly is entertaining. I try to imagine how it is enjoyable to others. I think I am sort of missing the game connection in my brain. I've practiced enough, believe me. I like word games or visually interesting games better than board games. Playing pretend also is not entertaining to me. It's sort of silly to me. I don't enjoy being in a role or acting. I speak poorly so I don't socialize on this level. I also have poor body control. How is it possible for me to pretend I'm an astronaut or a doctor or whatever? I pace and flap and it's annoying to other kids.

I'm too old now anyway and it's good because I hated my pretend drills in ABA. I had a script and I had figurines of farm animals and I had to put them in the toy barn. No pretend at all, just scripted play. I have imagination. I write creative stories and I think of stories in my head. I can do that with my poor speech and body control. The problem is that many specialists in autism conclude I, and others, have no theory of mind because we don't play Star Wars or whatever. I guess they have trouble imagining why pretend is boring if you can't speak, control your body well, or initiate your ideas.

I think I can imagine their theories and how they reached their insights better than they can imagine smart, intact people trapped in a non-responsive body. I count myself lucky to have gotten myself out of my isolation. It's as if I was freed from a lonely desert island. The island had enough food and some supplies but they weren't the right supplies to get me off. It was horrible. I'd try to build a raft but it would turn into a table or a lamp. I mean, it was not addressing my needs at all. Only when my mom saw I could write did I see more hope, but the ship was too far from shore. Then, Soma helped me build a raft and my family improved the raft until it could float anywhere: at school, or at parties, or at dinner, or in a car. It is always helpful to build a raft that is seaworthy. I'd still be on my desert island with no raft if no one had given me communication, or exercise, or respect. I am living proof that communication is the key. Not lamps or tables that that look nice but keep me stuck on my island.

I guess I have some imagination because I imagined this. I'm not sure my experts can imagine my reality and I think they should get pretend drills to get more empathy and improve their theory of mind to at least my level.

Bad Behavior
May 2009

I spent so many years not fully present that it's easy for me to travel to my inner world of stims when I get stressed out. If I want to escape stress, all I have to do is go in my head to its highs of sensory lights. I get remote there because it's far from the real world, so I am sort of resisting work and not stopping my behaviors. In truth, it organizes me to write about and analyze my illness. I stopped writing recently because I thought my book was done and in no time I was going back to old behaviors I had not done in months. It's good to know I need to write about my feelings to have more self autonomy and self awareness. It's like a talking treatment. I need to exercise, piano, communicate and write to help me stay focused in reality. If not, I swirl internally in my inner life. So, so, so easy to return to but it's a prison to me so I don't want to return there. I must maintain my gains so I can defeat this inner lure to be stimmy so that I can try to make a normal life for myself. My progress is not in a straight line. As I write I see what I should work on. I will continue to write my journey for myself because now I see that writing heals me.

Communication Issues
May 2009

I realize that some questions remain unanswered. I am certain people will be most curious about my independence in communication. I have already explained how I need help to keep me on track. I am super-short-attention-spanned. My mind has to be rushing to this and that all the time. Internally I'm struggling to fight all my distracting thoughts and impulses. Every noise is a serious challenge to my focusing so I rely on others to help me with that. I wish I could say to my brain, "Stop whizzing around so much," but it is a losing battle. I need to accept my style of thought. It's always slowing down after I exercise so that's some relief. Still, I need help with attention and that's why someone is near me when I point or type or in school. But you must understand that they do not facilitate my writing. These are my own thoughts, not anyone else's.

When I use a letter board I don't hold it myself for a few reasons. First, I am not coordinated. It is hard for me to hold a letter board steady with my other hand. I have tried and I just can't do it. I get flustered. Even holding a book steady to read is simply out of reach. I am not able to hold it still for long and turning pages one at a time is awful. I prefer books on tape or read out loud to me for that reason. I am sad about this. I love to read but the words in my head compete with those on paper and I can't read the whole book that way. By that I mean that my head is full of written words all the time. I see every word spelled in my head in any language I know. Reading chapter books sends lots more letters into my system. It can be overwhelming sometimes, so I prefer to hear my literature.

I wish I didn't need to rely on others for external support so much, but I do, so I am resigned to it, but I continue to try to overcome it anyway. It's sort of a curse because we autistic people require so much support to function and to emerge from our silent prison that many people miss our potential and see only failure and limitations. In so many cases we are denied even minimal support in communication and so we can't emerge at all. It's so sad to see my friends be so misunderstood all the time.

In typing no one holds the keyboard at all but it has to sit on a table. I am adjusting to this and I'll become more skilled at it, but I still need a person nearby to help me keep my focus or I return so easily to my internal world which makes no demands and provides a drug-like trance to boot.

I was asked how I wrote this book, meaning how I composed my essays. I have thought about my illness for a long time. I have wondered about my behaviors and I have analyzed my actions for years, so much of it was composed in a way already. It was ready to be written and it flooded out of my hand in a kind of release.

Social Anxiety
May 2009

If I seem disinterested in people it's not because I have no skills or understanding of social behavior. It's due to shyness and anxiety. I'm so shy it is forever interfering with my ability to socialize. It's true I get overwhelmed sensorally but often I am overwhelmed in shyness. This causes me to withdraw or watch TV or stim. It's worst in groups. One-on-one isn't so hard. Unfortunately, it makes people think I am disinterested in others when it's the opposite. I care about people, but I am shy to the point of feeling better in hiding than in socializing. Add to that my speech and body control problems and you have even more causes to feel shy. It's not as bad as in the past. Then I'd really want to withdraw. At times when I was small I'd even hide in my closet, or inside my tee-shirt pulled over my face when I had to be around uncomfortable people I didn't know. Now I don't do that, but the anxiety remains.

I am worried that people will decide that I am so impaired that I'm not worth the effort. I understand that I don't have to prove to everyone that I am okay in my own idiosyncratic way. People either accept me or they don't. All shy people can empathize with me and my fears. I'm not alone in my social anxiety which is fairly common. The problem is how others interpret my shyness. In my case, experts deduce that because of my autism I'm not a social person and that I like objects more than people. This is a big misconception.

Imagine being stuck in silence with poor body control and anxiety that can be paralyzing. Doesn't social withdrawal make sense in this context? If the experts look only at external behavior, not the cause of the behavior, then it's clear why they assume I might not be interested in people. But people withdraw socially for different reasons: shyness, embarrassment, sadness, communication problems and anxiety, and this is true for normal people too. I would never conclude that shy people must prefer computers or books to people. They feel safer with them because these are not able to hurt their feelings. This is why an autistic person retreats inside stims or in hiding. The solution is patience, loving support and accepting and respecting the autistic person.

Under-Estimated
July 2009

A friend of mine who is really output-impaired got a painful bug bite. His mom remarked that the poor kid was suffering and couldn't understand why. I don't get how a parent can even assume this. How awful to hurt physically and add to that the emotional hurt of being thought to be so simple-minded that you can't understand why you are in pain. Every time I hear a story like this I feel a need to get my book out. This is an unnecessary misunderstanding and it is tragic.

It occurred to me that this loving mom felt this way because she has been taught that until her son can show that he knows something in his drills he doesn't have the concept. This is based on a learning theory that we learn best in steps and in a sequential order. If Drill One isn't mastered then all that follow lag behind, out of reach, and mastery is "proven" by accuracy in card pointing.

The mind isn't quite so linear, though. It has gaps, even in normal minds. For example, someone could be a math wiz and poor in learning languages, or a language wiz who stinks in math. My aunt complains that she has no sense of direction and she is always getting lost, but she is intelligent in other ways. If she had to master her deficit in directions before she could study music, or science, or geometry, we would think it ridiculous. In autism education that is exactly what happens. We can't learn science until we master our drills. We can't master our drills if our bodies don't listen to our minds' commands and so we are presumed to know nothing at all.

In my own case, when I was younger I had a teacher who told my mom that I didn't understand when I was bad that I had been bad. She told my mom that she should stop insisting that I fix my mistakes or apologize to others. She told her in front of me that making me apologize was not a good idea because I had no understanding of my actions and I had no understanding of what right and wrong was. It was a reprieve from responsibility and I liked that, but she was dead wrong. I knew exactly why my mom was angry with my behavior and it upset me that my teacher thought so little of my intellect.

The mind is a complex world we have only begun to explore. It is possible that someone can look odd, have a stimmy and non-responsive body, be unable to speak and still be intelligent. I believe the potential exists in my friend, as it existed in me before I could communicate.

A Kind of Paralysis
November 2009

I have been thinking a lot about my non-responsiveness. It is almost like a form of paralysis, except, thank God, I'm not paralyzed, but I still think it's like a paralysis of intentional responses. I am telling my hand to raise in class, or my feet to run, or my fingers to move on the piano, however they don't listen to me. Either they don't move, or they move badly. It's really rotten. I live in a world in which my brain is sort of only for thinking and my body needs guidance and can't get the input it needs from the brain. The brain guides stims which are stupid and pointless and only a distraction from life, not a tool to live by.

I'm not paralyzed to wave ribbons, or to pace, or things like that. Then I'm the opposite of paralyzed. I can't get my body to stop moving around, though I want it to. It's a true irony. I am getting my signals messed up. If I want to move, I'm stuck like a stump and my brain is thinking of what it wants my body to do. It ends there. Thinking, not responding.

In other words, what good is my free will if I am like a thinking man in a straight jacket? It seems a sad life wishing to move and knowing it's a gamble whether I have the connection or not to allow me to do so at that moment. I am throwing the dice in the air—react, not react, or stim I can't stop. If I win, I do the thing I want. If I lose, I'm a stump, or an uncoordinated semi-stump, or forced to do involuntary stims.

These are my options and I hate it. It improves with fitness and exercise but so slowly I don't think I will ever have control of my body in the way I want. I fight the temptation to despair because I really want to free myself. It's my job to free my soul. Hopefully one day my body will be free too.

Language Processing
December 2009

It's a misconception that non-verbal autistic people are not processing language. As I have mentioned, I understood everything as a non-verbal autistic child. The erroneous theory is this: to speak is to understand. Tell that to Stephen Hawking.

It's not fair to assume that because non-verbal autistic people have no means to convey their thoughts that they think in a limited way. Even some verbal autistic people claim this. It's not a language processing problem. It's a motor problem. Soma is teaching us how to communicate the thoughts that we thought in silence before. She didn't teach us to process language, nor did my ABA flashcards. She helped me find a way to get out what was already in me.

I am sure that as more and more attitudes adapt to this new information many autistic kids will suddenly recover from their receptive language processing deficits. Ha ha.

Recognizing Danger
December 2009

Why do children with autism seem to do dangerous things? Many experts claim we have no judgment. I don't know about that. I know I have bothered my parents many times by doing impulsive things. It's hard for me to stop my impulses. It's like not eating dessert or something you want times ten. You tell yourself no and you do yes.

I see typical kids do impulsive things too like doing dangerous tricks on bikes. It's not always stupidity or cluelessness. In autism it's another body control issue.

Traffic is visually stimulating. It may invite some kids to move toward it. I can't explain that one, but I have felt the impulse to bolt suddenly. It can be at a bad time but the impulse is so strong it can feel impossible to resist. It's not due to ignorance or idiocy. It is the impulses and too weak a body control to fight them off. It doesn't matter why. We still need supervision to be safe.

The Curse of Self Pity and the Gift of Autism
January 2010

I know how often I get stuck in self pity. I find that it's a lot easier to be miserable than to be cheerful, yet misery is no way to live. I think depression is a lot easier than optimism because to be optimistic takes effort when life is tough, and depression takes no work at all. It's interesting to see how one person's depression brings everyone around them down too. It's like a contagious illness, so we who are prone to sorrow need to work at it, if not to make our own lives better then to be kind to those who have to be with us. The question is what helps fight the tendency to self-pity and neediness?

It's not due to easier lives. My grandmother had a super hard life but she is cheerful most of the time. I think a lot of it has to do with expectations. If you think life owes you something, you can't appreciate what you have. I always compared myself to typical kids. I'd limit myself in my jealousy and I'd see myself missing out on life's pleasures. I didn't see that they were not living perfect lives. They had typical brains, but maybe I had some things they didn't, like my home, or family, or my spirit.

The way to appreciate your good fortune is to notice your blessings. I feel lucky to communicate. I don't take it for granted. I am lucky to be more independent and stronger than I once thought I ever could be. I see that to hate your life dooms you to a wretched one, even if the life you have is hard. The truth is I don't need to be normal to make my life meaningful. I need to have freedom to think, loving friends and family, and a recognition that no life is perfect. In spite of an illness I wish I didn't have, I actually have it better than many people.

It's my job to fight my self-pity by remembering that it isn't all bad. In fact, as much as I hate to admit it, autism has given me a lot of good things too. In the silence I lived in I learned to think deeply about things. I learned to observe and to understand people and their emotions, and I see that my illness is not the end. It is only a challenge that I now know I can deal with. The secret to happiness must be in stopping self-pity.

Hero

February 2010

I met a real hero. How do I know he is a hero? He does brave things even if his own safety is in danger. He saved many lives in battle, in rescue operations, in bringing people to freedom from persecuted lands, in fighting against terrorism, and in fighting for disabled people.

How is it that one person takes on so much responsibility? It's hard to know where courage comes from but I think it's in all of us if we allow ourselves to be brave. I think some heroes assume that everyone would do what they did because it is normal to them to do amazing things. Others react in a moment without thought. Some are heroes once and others over and over again.

It is inspiring for me to meet a man who did not take the comfortable or easy path. He took another way. The truth is that heroes are made in situations that require exceptional people. If we can face our fears, we can do things we never thought we could. We need to see that heroes are sometimes scared or reluctant but they do what they have to because they decided to do it. It's not the hero gene. It's the hero decision, I think.

God and Suffering
March 2010

I was thinking about God and suffering. When we really need God is when we hurt inside. That is when God can seem like a remote presence. I often felt like God didn't hear my prayers because I didn't get better and it was my greatest hope. I prayed and God was not sending me a cure, so I got the idea that God didn't care about me.

It is a common reaction. It helps to see a response to a prayer because we tire of suffering and expect some relief. I think that God doesn't see it that way. He isn't helping just because we believe He should. He helps in His own way, in His own time, I think.

The religious person may feel betrayed by God, but God is there and listening to his prayers. God isn't a wish-fulfiller. He is a **hope**-fulfiller. He gives our soul an outlet for our hopes that would not be heard otherwise.

I spoke to God for a cure. He didn't cure me but He instilled in me a determination to help myself and other autistic people. He gave me a way to express my thoughts and to relate to people. He helped me see that autism is not the end of my hope but it is a challenge.

The truth is that all people face challenges at some point. The person who seems so happy on the outside may suffer inside. We all have sorrows—in the death of a loved one or an injury or a crime or a million other sorrows—some big and some small. The task we face is to keep moving and hoping. I mean, we have to find the strength to face our suffering and fight for life. We get our strength from our loved ones, but also in our hope that God guards for us. He helps us to know that we do not have to stay trapped forever. There is God's promise of a better possibility.

It's a hard struggle. I fight my doubts and my demons every day but I am so sure that hope is like a taste of God's presence. How else would we have this relief if not for God? I think horrible things seem worse without this hope that promises a better tomorrow. It's necessary to see that our suffering leads to calming hope through our love in God.

I also think we cope with suffering by forcing ourselves to see God's blessings around us. When we are suffering all we see is the pain in the world and in ourselves. I saw my suffering as the result of a cruel world. If I saw a nature film I saw the predator and the prey playing out a cruel system of winner/loser.

It's a lot more complicated than that, though it is a competition to survive, it's true. The animals don't kill for sport. They kill to live. In the animal kingdom a lion dies if it cannot hunt a zebra. The zebra dies if there are too many of them. There is a system that supports both a lion and a zebra in a kind of relationship of survival. I see it now not as cruel for the zebra but as enabling the herd to stay strong and live, so what I'm trying to say is that the world isn't only cruel. There may be a benefit to what seems miserable.

We get strong from fighting adversity. My situation has taught me to point on a letter board. It's slow. I need a lot of time to say what I want. On the other hand, I get to think about what I say and I don't waste my words. This is like funneling my thoughts into a clear stream. It's like a gift in a way though I hate the speech problem.

The truth is that much of what people say is meaningless. They instantly say what comes into their head. Their lack of working on their thoughts makes their thoughts unfocused. It's not only a curse to be quiet, it's a blessing of thinking inside and saying what is important, so a bad thing may be an opportunity too. It is our inner determination that keeps us feeling hopeful and enables us to turn suffering into an opportunity and a mission.

The world is full of sorrow and it's easy to find: illness, war, death, earthquakes and tsunamis, and just when you feel it's all sadness, it's spring and the world bursts into bloom and life is all around and it is like a miracle of life.

The world is joy and sorrow and we tend to see joy as our blessing and sorrow as our curse. We work for now to find joy or to preserve it, but the suffering we face is also part of the system of life. It is the suffering that forces the world to improve itself and it reminds us to appreciate the blessings we have.

Emotional Roller Coaster
March 2010

My emotions are like a force that takes over my entire self. It may be good feelings or bad. I get happy. Then I get so happy I roller coaster to goofy and I laugh or stim uncontrollably. This can feel sort of scary. It is taking over so quickly. I try to resist. It is like stopping a rolling boulder. It's more powerful than I am, so I roll with it. I can't stop it on my own. I need someone to calm me in some way. I need to walk or leave to have a return to my control. I am relieved if I return to control. It's overwhelming to be on an emotional roller coaster. I get so sad to be so stuck in my body at these moments. It is tempting to give up then.

On the other hand, I used to get so sad I would weep in sorrow for hours. It was the worst. I was drowning and I could not hear the person trying to help me. It was more than depression. The emotions were the same roller coaster only they were diving into sorrow instead of goofy happiness.

It is the stupidest illness. I am turning into an emotional roller coaster sometimes though I can't show my feelings on my face at will. I want to smile when I greet someone though I sit in blank expression, then when emotions are intense I show too much. It's lousy, though I will overcome some of it by practice. It's important because how I act affects how people treat me.

Mainstreaming
May 2010

I am mainstreamed in all my academic classes. I go to history, math and science in regular classes beginning in first period. I also get grade level work in English but I stay in autism class to do it. I have to get used to sitting quietly all day and I'm not ready for four mainstream classes. It is a skill to sit and listen. Since my body behaves erratically I mostly concentrate on self control. It is exhausting and I try to have good days as much as possible.

My attitude is the key. I attack the stims like a war but I fail sometimes. It's forced me to really see my behavior in terms of how others react to me. Sometimes I'm noisy and kids look at me. It's embarrassing and I hate that my control is so poor. It's not on purpose to be a jerk. It's only to get my feelings out. I have no nuanced outlet. It's hard to be subtle without good motor control. Though I see other kids talking and being disruptive, I know that they are not as disruptive as I am if I make noises.

I do all the same work and no modifications in homework or test content, though I sometimes leave the room or get more time to take tests because pointing is so slow. I am proud that I got a good report card this year. It took me a while to learn how to be in a regular class after all my years in a pre-school autism class. It makes me nostalgic for doing nothing all day. Ha-ha.

I mean, what a teacher teaches is everything. One teacher teaches me about cellular respiration and how life is structured in cells. Another teaches about the Renaissance and the state of affairs in medieval Europe, and another about algebra or math skills. Then there's what I had before this; finding toys in Play Doh, reviewing the day of the week and the weather every day, tearing my hair out from not learning a thing year after year and hoping that one day I'd be out of this torture. It is a real blessing to learn in school. I don't take it for granted.

I think I have to get used to being a pioneer. I was initially so self-conscious of bothering the other kids and embarrassed that I couldn't talk or be normal, but those are things I couldn't control at all. I had to accept myself in order to calm down and I was helped in therapy to accept my illness more. I am not so embarrassed now. I am proud that a horrible illness hasn't deprived me any more of my right to learn. I see my role generally as a sort of leader in autism in that I am trying to take non-verbal autistic people to a true education once and for all.

I get lonely in mainstreaming, to be sure. I don't fit in with typical kids because it's impossible to keep up in conversation, so I can't joke with them. I think of funny jokes all day but only I get to laugh at them.

Also, some kids my age are really insecure. Since I'm not normal I can't be status improving to hang with, so they irritate me in their rejection of me because I am so weird. They are normal. I live a harder challenge, but I don't really like shallow people at all.

Some kids have kinder hearts. They say "hi" and work in groups with me and treat me well. I am starting to feel more relaxed with typical kids so mainstreaming has made me interested in expanding my world. I need to live in the normal world. I can't hide in my autism social shell, only stimming and staying in an autistic class. That's restricting me from the life I want. The ticket out of my stuck situation was having the ability to communicate. Obviously autistic people without communication are not ready to be mainstreamed. The solution is not boring them to death. It's helping them to learn to communicate —hello. So in time, I won't be the only weirdo in my classes, I hope.

Nature
May 2010

I love being in nature. Noisy environments drive me mad inside. It's sort of terrible because I overload in my sensory system too easily. I can tolerate a baseball game with headphones on or eat in a restaurant. Not easy for me to cope with the din, but I do.

In nature it's just soothing sounds like birds or wind in the trees or ocean waves. It is like a reprieve from feeling haywire inside from noise and bustle. I also love the natural beauty of natural settings. We hike often in our local open space preserve with our dogs. It's so lovely there with rolling hills, oak trees, and native grass blowing in the breeze.

I love the ocean. I feel exhilarated there. The water is so cold. The sand is so warm and the salty smell is so nice. I watch the waves and I am transported into a sense of nature. It's so compelling but it also makes me get too lost sometimes because I also get so flappy.

I also have a deep love of the mountains. I am hardly ever happier than when we are in the mountains, hiking or kayaking or swimming in the mountain lakes. It is spiritual to be in a lake, floating in a kayak, surrounded by beauty. It reminds me that I'm small and insignificant in nature, yet part of it too. I sleep well in the mountains.

Accepting My Illness
May 2010

It has been a long ordeal to learn to accept my illness. I have tried to wish it away, pray it away, and imagine how my life would be without autism. This is a recipe for sorrow, let me tell you. Oh, I am so tired of living in a body I can't control, but I hate to admit I may never be able to. Therefore I'd better accept my reality and move on. This assumes I can accept something I hate. But not accepting means I'm trapped in misery.

I see other people who have accepted their challenges bravely. I have a cousin who injured his spine in his first year of college. He is paralyzed from the waist down. I see how he has moved on and finished college and is an athlete at a high level in a wheelchair sport. I try to move on in the same way. It's harder in some ways because I'm not physically disabled. I'm neurologically, internally really screwed up. I see my goals and my body refuses to listen so often.

I feel more at peace though about it now. I think I need to work more on accepting myself the way I am. If I don't, I'm still this way, just sadder. I see my body getting better in work outs. This gives me hope. I was out of shape, like most autistic people. Not anymore and I intend to get stronger. It's a decision and I have to believe I can have a quality life with a terrible illness. I attack the doubts. I must win. I see that.

It's an interesting thing. All the world admires people who overcome disabilities, like Helen Keller, Stephen Hawking or the athletes in the Paralympics. Where did they get the will to fight the sadness and achieve? They had to decide to live the way they are, to be ready to try even when it's hard, to have courage to be different, to turn a trial into an achievement.

I am sure Helen Keller had bad days and despaired sometimes. She still triumphed. She never was cured. She didn't ever see or hear, but she made an impact on the world. She showed that a solitary confinement in silence and sightlessness, with determination and the right teachers could not stop her from being free.

I may never lose this illness but I'm getting closer to accepting it as part of me. I will continue to work on it because I need to be happy. If I accept that I can exercise, practice the piano, and write and this helps me improve my mood and skills, then it is a lot. I don't need a miracle cure to live well, but I must persevere in trying, like my cousin did.

It seems overwhelming to struggle so much, yet what is the alternative? If I stay in sorrow I'm truly doubly trapped because on top of my illness I am sad. I think how I face my illness is key. It isn't necessary to like having autism to accept it.

I wish I was fine. I wish I didn't have to struggle so much. I wish I could talk. I wish my body obeyed my mind. I wish a lot, but I KNOW I can triumph over my limitations. I mean to live a quality life in spite of a big challenge.

It's so important to conquer self-pity in order to do that. The world will have to meet me halfway. The first step is to accept me for an intact mind and soul. Then it will be my job to do what needs to be done to live fully.

It's more than that, though. I see teenagers struggle to accept and like themselves every day. They don't have autism or any illness I can see but they make themselves so miserable trying to have a cool image. It's interesting because they can't like themselves the way they are if they are desperate to fit in with a group that doesn't accept them as they are.

It means they must conform to a standard that has nothing to do with who they are, but rather, what they wear or how they talk—like swearing constantly—or music or even whether they do homework or not. So my struggle to accept my illness that makes me an outsider at this age of wanting to fit in is even tougher. Nevertheless, the only thing to be done is to start figuring out how I want to live. We can take time to investigate our own nature to decide who we are and how we want to live.

I'm determined to live like anyone else in that I want friends, work, and to get as much better as I can. My life is mine, so I have to accept what it has in it that I'm powerless to change, to overcome what I can, and see how much happier I am now than I ever was in the past.

It's not helpful to mope about the things that are there, impossible to change. I mean, my cousin became a wheelchair mountain biker, not a conventional mountain biker. He couldn't change his injury, but he could control his attitude towards it. In the times I have seen him he is independently driving, not asking for anyone's help or pity, and embracing life from a wheelchair. He may not have picked that life but it picked him. So the choice was isolation and self-pity or get out there and deal.

It's true in life. There are people who paralyze themselves from moving on. It's all internal. I mean, one emotional hurt and they quit. This can be selfish because it affects their loved ones. I've seen a lady I know who has given up, and I see how it hurts her family. So she is indulging in her self-pity at their expense. If it sounds harsh, it should.

On the other hand, I saw a friend of my sister's yesterday. Her beloved father died a few months ago after a brief illness and she is embracing life, and keeping busy, and being pleasant to be with. That is courageous, I think. She saw that her life wasn't over though she had a big loss. We choose to accept or not in order to move on or stay stuck.

My illness is a challenge twenty-four hours a day. I long for a reprieve, yet I know I am conquering a lot. I can do more. I can communicate now. I can exercise my body and my mind. In time I will improve to the level I can take it, but I must accept that autism is a part of me. So, I see that autism gives me not only challenges but a few good things too.

It gave me a goal in life to help others like me to break free of theories that trap us. It gave me the ability to analyze and think things through in all my silent years. And, it gave me the courage to write this personal book because it's a story that hasn't been told yet in autism books. Out of my autistic mind may come a curiosity to get autism researchers looking at new ideas, parents providing real communication to kids, teachers really teaching stuff—no more flashcards, no more "No, try again"—to kids like me, no more being treated as stupid by lots of kindly but patronizing people. This hope allows me to accept my reluctant membership in Autismland, but it also gives me the strength to live as I am.

Overwhelming Impulses
May 2010

I'm a strange mixture. I am smart as a mind and dumb as a body. I can think of insights and my body ignores them. I can write of intelligent ideas and my body acts on non-thinking impulses. It's embarrassing and discouraging and I hate it.

I live in a world of high thoughts and primitive impulses. So I impulsively pour things down the drain or open things I shouldn't because I follow my body in those moments. My mind tries to stop me. It is overpowered. I regret my actions afterwards but that doesn't change what I did.

It's worse if I'm tired and sick or weak in some way. Now I see it is robbing me of my freedom to live normally. Normal people don't get these horrible moments of compulsion. Sure, they eat too much and things like that, but they don't pour colorful things down the drain, and things like *that*.

Today, I was on a roll. I poured mouthwash in the sink, shaving lotion on the mirror, and salt scrub in my room. It's hard to say why. I obey.

That's all.

What I need to do is fight harder. I fight my body non-stop anyway. If I didn't I'd be getting into even more trouble, so I need to try, especially when the obsessions make me weak. If I can overcome the compulsive behavior I'd be in a good place.

Moses, Disabled Hero
May 2010

Moses couldn't talk well yet he was the man God selected to liberate the Hebrew slaves. Why did God choose an imperfect man to do the job? Moses pleaded with God to choose someone else. He said, "I don't talk well. How can I speak to Pharaoh? How do I make my point heard?" God insisted it be Moses in spite of his speech disability. "Moses," he told him, "you must use your brother Aaron as your spokesman."

Why did God do this? I think for several reasons. First of all, Moses was a great man, perfect in spirit and values. He fought for justice. He yearned for fairness, and he was a free soul inside. He was a slave's son *and* a prince. He knew freedom and he was not limited by fear of the whip.

I think God also wanted to show that perfect in His eyes is not the same as perfect in man's. That is, God looks to the core, not the shell. Moses was not sure he could do it because he saw the shell. The core was revealed gradually as he led the slaves to freedom.

Moses amazed the world in his challenges. Who was he, this speech impaired shepherd, to challenge Pharaoh, thought to be an embodiment of the gods at that time? Moses assumed he was right when he insisted on freedom because God insisted it was right. Pharaoh assumed he was right when he insisted on slavery because no one dared challenge Pharaoh. That is, until Moses, the reluctant spokesman, stuttered and Aaron repeated the command to let the slaves be freed.

Moses taught the world that God rejects slavery. No matter how this idea has been ignored, no one can honestly argue after the Exodus, that God approves of enslaving others. This was the first time that humanity saw a mass liberation movement and it has inspired people for thousands of years to aspire to be free.

There is also a lesson in mutual support. Moses had a helper, and this, I think, shows that we should not take too much on alone. Aaron and Moses are a team. I am sure Aaron needed Moses as much as Moses needed Aaron, and God relied on both of them to convey his instructions of liberation.

The message of Moses is that one leader doing what is right, with the right support, can change a terrible situation to one of hope and promise. I get inspiration from Moses. I faced a terrible situation without hope in my childhood. But, despite my inability to speak, I have reluctantly seen that if I don't say the truth it may be years before change occurs. So, I face *my* pharaohs—autism experts—to see if we can't find a way to liberate autistic people from the solitude they face.

Age 14, Motivation

In this year I continued to educate others about autism, do more speeches, and to help people with autism and their families. I saw hope and possibility more and more, and I realized that by improving my own self-control and skills, and by accepting myself, I could better achieve my goals. This helped me to become a happier person.

Onward, Upward
May, 2010

I am satisfied with more and more in my life. The truth is our attitude
helps with the way we help ourselves deal with adversity. If I am open
to challenges, don't give in to sorrow and have a goal in mind, I can
do in time what seems now out of reach. I see it daily. I can go far, I
believe, if I am determined. In autism, just simple tasks seem impossible.
So, instead of trying, we tell ourselves to stim our severe frustration
away. Stims are the drug of the trapped. We can't do what we would
like our bodies to do but God gave us this self-soothing hallucinatory
escape from reality. I felt I couldn't live a positive life but I could live
a hallucinatory sensory experience just fine. I've stimmed away years
of my life.

I stim so much less now that I can communicate. I don't need to
escape as much because I am starting to see a future for myself. I once
thought I'd be trapped my entire life in silence and stuck with no control
over my destiny. Thanks to my really good luck of meeting Soma,
having a satisfactory mind, the most amazing parents who insisted I
be a self-sufficient human-being, or as much as I could be, I am in
mainstream classes getting an education, writing a book, having friends,
getting in shape, giving speeches to audiences, going to sleep away
camp for a week, doing chores like making my own bed and folding my
laundry (even if I still need help). I see light where once I saw darkness.

My amazing dad has filled my life with new challenges and fun. He
is responsible for helping me sit quietly in a restaurant and to tolerate
baseball games and even a concert. I shop in stores and it's hard to
control my impulses, but I have to try or I don't do better. I don't
know what my future will be, but I know it won't be a stimming person.

It's like this: if we work then we improve, no matter how slowly or
how hard. But we must work on the right things. I may be saying it too
much, but flashcards are not the work we need. Sensory integration
and swings don't help if I can't do anything bilateral. If I have trouble
crossing my midline in exercise I can't do much, right? Why did my
mom have to figure this out and not any of the professionals we saw

all these years? Well, at least she saw it, so I'm learning to triumph over my body thanks to my getting the greatest trainer ever. I will always be grateful to him.

When I was eight I was depressed and hopeless. I just turned fourteen and I'm telling you I'm actually excited about my future. If I could, I'd cure this rotten illness. Since I can't, I will help triumph over it. I see and understand that my illness is for the birds- ha ha- so I'd better take off and fly.

Memory Triggers
May 2010

I had an interesting experience today. I worked out with two volunteer athletes at an activity that had special needs kids meet with college students. At first they talked to me in simple tones and words, though they were very nice. This horrible memory of patronizing ABA words of "good job" triggered turmoil in me. It's weird. I hear a kindly meant "good job" and I get goosebumps and I feel myself back in my room, at my table, looking at flashcards I can't answer accurately.

It's an awful thing. I'm obviously still so affected by those memories. If I hear, "no, try again" or "high five" or "good job" I wind up in my room, at my table, trapped and miserable. My mom just told me it's like a Post Traumatic Stress Disorder. But, I'm not in my room anymore, and the table is long gone, and I don't have to look at flashcards, so I need to move on emotionally. Once the girls saw me point on my board and knew I was intellectually intact they treated me differently. I suppose it's natural to think an autistic person is slow, not profoundly stuck. It's the struggle of the silent to prove that still waters run deep and sometimes not the way that is assumed.

Recognition
May 2010

The IEP Committee last week determined that I will be mainstreamed all day next year, so I will no longer be a special education student. I will be a general education student. This is amazing from a School District that once denied I could even communicate. I am proud of this, though I get nervous too because the challenge is big. Soma took me on a journey from silence and doubt to inclusion and recognition. If not for her, I'd still be reading toddler books and not textbooks.

A Walk in the Woods
March 2011

I love nature. In nature I am teamed up with God, in a way. I mean, I look around. I see beauty all around me, and I feel part of it. The illness is put aside because I see perfection in the really lovely sights.

Nature isn't neat or orderly. The grass is waving this way or that. The branches are crooked and gray and gnarled. The path is lopsided from rivers of rain and erosion. The plants grow in random places. I see no pattern, unlike a landscaped lawn.

I fit in so well. I am so at home in the messy beauty of nature. I relate to it. I see the system is messy, but it works and it is WOW. I see my illness this way. It's not pretty. It is messy. It has erosion and rivers of mud too. But it is part of nature in the same way.

I am not a mistake, nor a sorry state of messy neurons. I accept my messy neurological system because it has given me a way of seeing life. I fit in with the path in the woods.

Emotional Overflow
March 2011

The struggle for emotional control is always with me. I try to meet the world on its terms. I need to calm myself to do that. It's not too bad if I feel OK inside. If I don't, oh boy. I find it is a train that rolls so swiftly that even if the engineer tries to stop it, the momentum keeps moving me onward. Once I stop I feel so embarrassed or sorry.

The triggers can be silly to others. Inside, they are serious.

I get nervous. It overflows. I get stressed. It overflows.

It overflows.

Oh man, do I hate that.

I behave the way people expect autistic people to act when I overflow, so they assume I'm not smart or something. Then I stop trying.

I think this is common for autistic people and it probably explains the tantrums some kids have. They tantrum from fear, anxiety or stress, but oh how quickly it becomes anger if people try to stop it with "hands down" or "no" or "all done" to a teenager.

The train is stopped by rules and understanding.

Dogs and Autism
March 2011

My dogs are a lot of fun. I am really glad we have them. When I was a baby we got a dog, so I am used to dogs. My home is always wagging and scampering.

They bother me when they bark, but it's bearable mostly. I still cover my ears sometimes because I hear too sensitively. It's worth it because I love them. They are patient with my annoying stims.

I know too many autistic people who scream in fear at the sight of dogs. It sort of makes sense because so many autistic people have sensitive hearing. Dogs are also full of surprises and they run and play in unpredictable ways. For me they have been an exercise in tolerance because I learned to love them in spite of their noise and their weird systems that make a sleeping dog jump out of its bed barking madly and running after some random sound it hears. This stresses some people, I'm sure, but I got used to it, times three. Maybe my dogs helped me in some ways to deal with a changeable world.

Autism and the Bossy Women
March 2011

Women who think they know it all have filled my life.

Wow, do I sound sexist? Not meant to be sexist. It's another rant.

From my home program as a little kid, to my OT therapists, to my speech therapists, to my teachers, to many of my evaluators, I have been bombarded with experts who have talked about me with such conviction, who assumed they were right, and who, in many cases, were not. They have almost always been women, for some reason.

It isn't really fun to have them make assumptions that minimize me and patronize me. I get livid because as a young kid, when I couldn't communicate at all, I had to listen to my wonderful women telling the world wrong insights and I knew my life would be worse because they had power over me in my education and so on, and I was stuck. I'm not stuck now. Getting communication and being respected is a terrific thing.

But these women somehow keep popping up. Thank goodness I know so many great open-minded women now, and some who after meeting me really open their minds after that, so it's not a sexist rant and it's not a stereotypical rant, but it is a true thing.

Think about it. The vast majority of my professional experts have been women who are super opinionated. And I encountered a new one this week. They listen only grudgingly to me or my parents, so sure they are of themselves. I simmer and boil and imagine analyzing them and planning their futures as they do for me, but instead I'll grin and make fun of them in my book.

Noticing Our Blessings
March 2011

Life is hard to predict. Even harder to count on. Since horrible things can happen without warning, I think we really need to live each day like it is a gift. Inside I get sad and edgy and I know I must fight it. My limitations irritate me so much. I lose myself in rotten resentment. Bad idea. I'm not helping my life in self-sorrow. I stop seeing my blessings in those moments, but I have so many blessings. I just have to notice them.

I may be disabled and non-verbal, but I am lucky too. I have a good family. I am cared for by many people. I have free will to communicate and to learn. I am loving my liberation inside as I climb out of autism's silence. I am into nature and music. God gives me breath each day.

Can I feel gratitude for the small miracles too? I must because small miracles add and add and add to a great gift. Living in recognition of our gifts is a weapon against sorrow. Those of us who get sad often must focus on our blessings.

I love delicious food and I'm lucky I have tastebuds to enjoy it. I love water and I'm lucky to swim. I love music and I enjoy it every day. Should I focus only on my illness and feel miserable? No, not ever. We must choose life in the belief we can make it better.

It is easy to make life worse and hard to make it better. But if our life is precious to God, which I believe it is, then I must see it is an obligation to be good to our own selves as well as others. The belief that it must be perfect to appreciate our gifts is sort of juvenile. I'm hoping to get better at this.

I see some disabled people who fight so incredibly bravely. I am so inspired by their attitude. I see how they fight on and on. I see it and I know it's not easy for them, but do they really have another good option? There is another option, but it stinks. Anger, resentment, and self-pity are horrible options. I think if we have one chance with our lives, we'd better live to our best in spite of our challenges.

Disabled or Super Able?
March 2011

I have been thinking about people with disabilities who succeed at high levels. For example, I wrote about Oscar Pistorius, the runner. He has no legs and he is a runner of world class speed. This is what we call a paradox.

In music, we find the same situation with Evelyn Glennie. She is a great musician and she feels her music because she is deaf. Look at what Beethoven accomplished in his deaf years.

In the sciences, we have Stephen Hawking. In engineering, Temple Grandin. In athletics, Jim Abbott (another paradox, a handless pitcher); and one-legged wrestling champ, Anthony Robles.

In other words, we have the human spirit unwilling to quit. Kind of staggering in a way because they had to fight very hard to be average. But they were not average. They were superior.

Adversity can make you determined. I know this from experience. Heaven knows, I'm a paradox too. I can't speak and I give speeches often. Someone else reads it out loud, and I'm standing near, but I'm not quitting. The inspirational and determined, who are shattering limits, are my hope and my models.

Sensory and Emotionally Overwhelmed by Well-Wishers
April 2011

Today I gave a speech before about a hundred women. I was nervous. I always am, even though I am used to giving speeches. I spoke about issues that are important to me; my personal mission of changing the way non-verbal autism is understood, how I want to be talked to (normally), how the community needs to be more accepting, and many other themes.

It was well received. It was the overwhelming aftermath I want to discuss. So many lovely, caring women rushed to me, hugging and kissing me. It was too much and I was overwhelmed. How can I explain it and not sound whiny?

My system is overly sensitive. Really, I am struggling all the time to be in control of myself. In emotional moments it is harder. Giving a speech, women who weep at my speech, teens who sob in my arms after my speech, so many questions people bombard me with in an instant... I wrote in the past about how I overflow. So, I did. I got aggressive in an instant, in front of my "admirers." I grabbed my mom and pulled her hair.

I love my mom and I don't have any desire to hurt her. I didn't, but she was livid all the same. I need to get better self-control. A friend of mine suggested that my mom should whisk me out after future speeches before the crowd gets up. Yes, I am pretty sure I need that. It's necessary if I'm going to continue doing speeches in person. I think seeing me in person helps people to believe my message.

If you have an autistic kid, this may help you understand the overflow you see. I do my best, but I am not normal neurologically. I believe it will improve, but meanwhile I have decided that I'm outta there the moment the speech is done. If there are questions, the audience can write to me at facebook or on my blog.

The lovely women are doting and I am fleeing. I greatly appreciate their good wishes more than they can know, but I need to go sooner.

My Poetry Recital
April 2011

I had to recite a poem out loud in my English class to be graded on flair, poise, memory, etc. Let me tell you how it went. A verbal recital is kind of a joke for me because I have mostly unintelligible speech and the flair of a tree stump. No attitude of drama. I can tell you the whole assignment felt silly. My mom suggested to the teacher that I use my computerized keyboard device with voice output in class to recite the poem. Then after class, one on one, I could spell it for the teacher on my letter board to show I memorized it. I thought that was a logical and fair accommodation.

My teacher said no. I needed to go in front of the class and spell the whole damn thing. So I tried. Stupid of me. I should have sat it out, to just get a "fail" because of my speech impairment. I spelled several lines. I like the poem, "Stopping By Woods on a Snowy Evening," by Robert Frost.

I got to line three and couldn't take the stress of the class staring at me. I felt so weird, so stuck, so disrespected by this teacher. It was overflow. I did what I hate time after time in overflow, which is really rare, but it happens. I can't control myself. I'm ashamed to say that I pulled my aide's hair in front of the entire class of about forty or so kids.

I feel wretched and remorseful. On the other hand, if my teacher had been sensitive to my disability, none of this would have happened. I learned an important lesson to say no if I can't do something, so maybe something happened in spite of my miserable performance that will help me in life.

Anxiety
April 2011

So very nervous inside all the time. That's what Temple Grandin says. That's the way it is for the majority of autistic people. Really, I overflow hoping I can control the stress I feel. The stress is so vicious inside. Even with communication and better skills I still suffer from it sometimes.

You see it in so many autistic people. They bolt or dash out. They stim because it soothes them. I see kids who bite and hit themselves, who scream and have meltdowns, not to get anything, but to have an outlet. These are the reasons why: severe nervousness, stress, internal overflow.

You can imagine how rough this is for people who can't communicate their ideas and feelings. They get told, "hands down" or "no" or people think they are not really aware of their emotions. Well, it is a bit different. It is sort of like a car rolling down a hill. It gains acceleration as it rolls. Think of that in an emotional sense.

What can you do to help? Quick removal from the stressful situation. If you need to come back, OK. The interruption is helpful in breaking the momentum. Also, it helps to get some caring. I remember seeing a non-verbal boy I know starting to get restless and really angry in a music lesson. His behaviorist was saying all the ABA things, "Hands quiet," "All done," and so on. It was getting worse. My mom was watching and she said to the boy, "I know it is so frustrating when your body doesn't do what you want it to."

You know what happened? He relaxed. That's what happened. Then he leaned on my mom to communicate his gratitude because he had no other way to express himself. This was important for me. Sort of a reminder that being treated with respect and kind empathy helps reduce anxiety, even in a kid everyone labels as "low-functioning."

Starting High School
April 2011

I was thinking how sorry I am to leave my middle school for high school. Well, not sorry exactly. I'm nervous and excited. I will be the pioneering non-verbal autistic person in regular education in high school. In middle school I wasn't the only autistic kid. I was the only one in my classes though. It's a long journey from my rudimentary autism class in elementary school to regular education in high school. It's really weird in a way because I am so stuck in my silence, however I am not trapped in it like I was. I can communicate in my typing/ pointing techniques and I am out in the world because I can express my ideas.

In high school I will have to really work hard on self control, on homework, on sitting all day, on proving myself once again. Now it is becoming easier. I'm nervous, not stressed to my roof. I think I can do it, and get my diploma, and even go to college. This is my goal and I hope it will help other autistic people on their journeys too.

Age 15, High School, for Bad and Good

High School is a dream I am living now. Just having the chance to learn and to be welcomed in a friendly and tolerant general education high school is awesome. It has been a journey because I discovered that not all educational systems are open or healthy, as you will read.

Nervous About Starting High School
May 2011

In a few weeks I will graduate middle school and next year I will start a new school. It's a big deal in my life. My middle school was the first real opportunity I had to learn in school. I know sixth grade was like an experiment. They watched to see how I could cope in middle school. I went in to math and science only, and did regular work in the other subjects though I wasn't mainstreamed in them then. It was a very big adjustment to sit so long in self-control and quiet. The schoolwork was simple compared to the work of sitting in a classroom all day. I was determined to get a decent education, so I tried. It was not always easy for me or my aide, but I got more capable each year. This year I am doing better. I am mainstreamed practically from eight to three. I go to P.E. with autistic kids, but otherwise I am staying in a regular class all day. My school is big. I switch rooms.

Next year my high school will be bigger still. It has about four thousand students, so many clubs I couldn't believe it, and a track and football field. It is a real big school experience. It's scary for new freshmen, I know. I'm really nervous. I worry that my sensory system will be overloaded. I worry that students will be mean to me. Then I tell myself, "OK, it's just worries and I am going to be fine." I will be with some kids I know. I can walk in the halls five minutes early to avoid the mob, but I can't stop my worries.

My aide is the best. It's wonderful to work with her. She is kind, smart, and good at working with me. I don't know her plans next year. I hope she can stay to start me off, or even longer. Now I worry that getting a new aide and a new school will be too much. Some days I get overwhelmed by worry. I wish I didn't, but I do.

I worry about the teachers. Will they accept me or think I am an odd nuisance to them? I worry about the students. Now I am in class with kids who are used to me. Next year there will be new kids. In middle school I visited school before the year started to meet all the teachers and tour the campus. That helped a lot and I hope to do that in my high school too. I also wrote a short speech that is read to the class on the first day of school to explain my behavior and communication style to the class. That helps put them at ease, but I am still so nervous inside.

I realize I am lucky. It's a great high school. It's a dream of mine to graduate and go to college. I will need to overcome my fears about high school. It's a big shift in my life. It's the third big change I've had in school. I went from remedial class in elementary school to a "high functioning" autism class in fifth grade. Then in sixth grade I went to my middle school. This time I really don't need to prove I'm smart to a school of skeptics. I think I've done that, so that is one big relief to me. It's wonderful that they believe in the need to educate me, so I no longer need to worry about that.

I feel next year could be good. Unfortunately it's unknown, so I worry too much. I feel relieved to write this.

Thanks to My Middle School
June 2011

The middle school I just graduated from was big. The procession in the graduation went on for about twenty minutes. It was an endless parade of students in suits or fancy dresses and high heels. The graduation meant a lot to me because I earned it. I thought about my journey to this point. I think I need to say thanks to the school.

In my education, I never had the chance to show my knowledge until middle school. It was the first school that accepted me as a student who could learn at grade level. They accepted me as a person who was different but not who needed to be kept from regular education. Each year got better and quickly became a full day of mainstreaming. When I started I wasn't sure I could do it. Now I know I can. I am starting high school with the knowledge that I did well in middle school.

My teachers were taking on a new kind of student. Classes were humongous. I got minimal individual attention. My classes were interesting or boring, like any other student's experience. It was normal boring, not a mind numbing denial of education boring. I am grateful to my middle school for that. Some teachers understood me and my situation better than others. Some were not very insightful at all. Some were open-minded and some were probably annoyed to have a disabled student crowding their classroom with an aide. The truth is, they all gave me a chance. Some people really never have this opportunity. It was hard, but a great thing to learn and be part of regular classes.

I think some people were amazingly helpful so I want to acknowledge them. First, I want to give special thanks to my wonderful aide, Cathy, for the patience of a saint, her lovely disposition, reliability, and wonderful communication skills. I also want to thank Mr. Miller who was always the problem solver and support I needed in administration. Last, thanks to Mrs. Johnston who in a short time became a huge help to me in my journey toward high school. The rest of the teachers simply deserve recognition for putting up with me.

Autism, Other People and Discipline
July 2011

How do you treat people with autism? In my experience the way people act can vary widely. Some people stare or act like I'm invisible. Others try to be nice. These fall into two groups. First are the ones who act like I don't understand anything and who look at me like I'm a species of lower-cognition human. They try to help by talking slowly and giving me high-fives. They are well intended. I am not angry at their not knowing and being kind. I do get angry if they know I understand and still act this way.

The other folks act pretty normally around me and ignore my weird stims when they come. I am so relaxed around these people. I do take advantage of the opportunities I get with people who are too understanding of me, however. If someone is not intuitive and I feel they are clueless, I can be a real pain, to put it mildly. I mean, all I need is a weak, sympathetic helper and I'm a strangely obnoxious guy.

It gets awful because I don't like being so stimmy and all, but I take advantage of the opportunity time after time. I laugh now thinking of the hapless substitute aide two years ago, who talked to me like I was not intelligent, watched me stim without helping me get control over myself, and told my mom I had a "good day" at school. When my aide returned the next day the assistant principal stopped her and said, "Never be absent again." Ha ha ha. It's funny now, if not then.

This is true in a way for all people. My history teacher was really structured. The students were sitting and working quietly. It was a really nice class. My English teacher was not good at structure or discipline. The same students were rude and disruptive. That class was more of a trial. My impression now is that a good leader is essential in teaching and in people who work with me. It's a true thing even with dogs, or anything. We work on making sure our dogs are not the leaders of our home. I know people whose dogs run the entire house.

In autism, we have impulse control problems. My aide must help me control impulses, keep me focused, and help me function in society. I am improving in self control. Glad about that, but I'll tell the truth, I'm likely to take advantage of wimpy people and I bet your autistic kid will too.

The Hope-Fulfiller
July 2011

I am religious inside like many people with my condition. Autism creates a sort of really deep spiritual connection to God. I see it in many people I know who have autism. My knowledge of religion is intuitive in some ways. I see so many people grapple with faith but I don't need to. I feel the presence of God and it gives me hope.

In my silent years I was dialoging internally all the time with God because He was filling my lonely days with hope. I saw early that God wasn't a wish-fulfiller because however much I prayed inside to be cured I was never out of my Autismland. I was sad in the feeling that God didn't care and I was feeling even abandoned. I was five or six then.

I started to be able to communicate at seven, and it is always getting better. I see I am not abandoned. Now my insights are more mature, not magical. I see God as a hope-fulfiller, not a wish-fulfiller. He fills me with hope and listens to my dreams and my prayers. I think that is for me the most important thing. I mean, if I didn't have a place to put my hopes, I would burst.

We, in Autismland, are socially isolated, and even if we have loving friends and families, it's not the same as a typical person due to our lonely illness that makes the outside world overwhelming and isolates people from us. Inside we are imagining our words and behavior and outside we are not able to do it the way we want. Frustrating lives. Sort of alone in company.

Alone is not always bad because I am good at thinking and philosophizing. Here I dialogue with God also, so, no matter what, I have a companion to sit with me. In a way autism creates a spiritual roadmap, insights, and an awareness of a holy entity that I see many typical, non-autistic people missing. The blindness of neuro-typicals is to miss the spiritual too often, and my blindness is in self control. I guess I have to be grateful for this pipeline that autism has given me to a rich relationship in faith and not just empty rote actions. The isolation is like a monk in a Trappist Monastery, silent but thinking. It's a sort of quiet relationship to have a walk with God. But I do, and I'm grateful.

On to High School
August 2011

Next week I go to a huge high school. It is intimidating. Still, I am so thrilled to have the chance to go. I think often how lucky I am to have escaped autism education. It was well-meaning, so I feel no anger about bad intentions. But however good the intentions, the result was stagnation in insufferable boredom. How many times must I do my schedule or read the same stupid words over and over? The days were repetitive. I learned nothing academic, so the journey I have been on for four years is the beginning of the true education of Ido.

I understand the school has to accept a disabled kid by law. Public school is a welcome doorway for me to have a chance to learn. I worked very hard to get to the point to go to regular high school. I realize I am at a crossroad in my life. I intend to work hard and earn this opportunity.

I am not under any illusions that the school is thrilled to have a seriously disabled student. I am a challenge. I am expensive because I need an aide. But I am a student who is pioneering opportunities for the disabled too. I am doing the same work as all the other kids so I don't expect charity or pity, only I hope to get tolerance, sensitivity to my situation and fair treatment. The doors open on Monday, and I'll try my best.

Envy is Lousy
August 2011

"If I didn't have autism..." is a phrase I realize is filled with turmoil. If ever I imagine my life as I wish it was I get so blue, so it's better to focus on what it is, not what it isn't. I have moments when I envy my sister or cousins or friends. I wish I could socialize with ease like they do. I wish I could be trusted alone. I wish I could learn to do things I can't, like sports or singing. I hope I don't sound whiny, but I see what I wish all day and it hurts sometimes. Still, I will keep persevering because I am determined to not waste my life in negative envy. Autism is a challenge I will deal with.

I keep thinking how hard the fight is. I know I have to fight, so I won't mope. I will see my work to the end, though I realize the end is always out of reach. It's true my illness is a trial at times. I can't wish it away any more than an amputee can wish his legs back. The solution is to fight envy and deal with what is, not what might have been.

Acceptance in High School
August 2011

High School is different than middle school. It is a lot bigger, to be sure. The teachers treat us more like mature people than kids. I have huge classes and it is a long walk between the buildings. I can deal with that.

Now I will explain what I can't deal with. I had an aide who was new, never worked in a high school before, nervous, tense, rigid, sort of made me feel like she was scared of me, and who seemed to wish she wasn't there. It was not a good thing for me. I need a calm, relaxed, supportive person to help me relax and feel less anxious, not someone who makes me feel even more tense. (Thankfully, I will have my old aide back next week for a few more months.)

I can't deal with the one-hundred plus degree temperature either. Lunch, nutrition, and P.E. are like saunas. I try to imagine swimming in an icy lake. It doesn't help. I am red and sweaty all day. It makes it all harder.

The hardest thing, though, is attitude. Not the students. They mostly ignore me. Not the teachers, except one. It is the administrators in special education, and I know they are scrutinizing my every move. In my last school I felt welcome. No one stood behind me with a notepad taking notes on my behavior. I felt confident they trusted I was in the right place. Not now.

Imagine how it feels to know that every behavior is documented by people who clearly think, "Oh my God, what is *he* doing here?" Then they wonder why I lose it. I was totally aware that my actions were being counted, listed, and collected as provable data that I am not good for regular education.

Which class do I lose it in? The one with the man who stares at me, stands behind me taking notes, and tells me I will never graduate. Is he not able to understand his presence is terrifying me?

I want so much to do well. I can't stop my autism to please his data collection. I wish I wasn't autistic so I could be anonymous in the eyes of administration. I can't do that unfortunately. I have to make myself not care that they would rather I leave or magically get cured.

I know I'm a seriously disabled guy. I have lived my whole life in the silence and isolation and impulsivity and the being misunderstood that autism brings. I have overcome a lot. I want a true education. I want a school that welcomes me. I hope I will succeed in this.

Letter to My Teachers
September 2011

Dear Teachers;

I started High School with several big challenges. The challenges are why I am easily the most different kid you have in your classes. I have a serious neurological difference. Recently a neuroscientist I know told me that it is theorized that autistic people have a surplus of neurons. Our brains don't prune properly. The result is a communication interference between thought and action. This is why I don't speak with my mouth or why my writing is messy. It is also why I am impulsive or emotional with poor brakes. It is awful for me to sometimes be the follower of my actions. I am struggling daily to master them.

The second challenge is attacks of anxiety. In autism we often are anxious, nervous and worried. That's when things are good. In real stress we sometimes are overwhelmed. Starting high school was really overwhelming and I lost my self-control. I am trying so hard to do well and I hope you see I am improving. I regret any disruption I caused and I will try to be a more relaxed student in the future.

One additional stress was that I was not with the right aide at the start of the school year. I think I need to work on finding good matches who help me stay calm. I have this now with Cathy. I did not have that before so I became stressed and even frightened.

I want you all to know that my education is a thing I value very much. It is challenging to be the only autistic kid like me in school. I know other students have autism but they are verbal or with less severe symptoms. Now I struggle to show that people like me can be educated too. I think the vast majority of people with my degree of autism have only a simple and very basic education of alphabet, arithmetic, and not much more. It was my good fortune that I was able to learn to communicate on letter board or computer with my one finger. Thanks to that, my education is possible. It liberated me from total isolation.

I know you are all busy and I appreciate you welcoming me to your classes. I realize you may get worried about whether I do my own work. I do all the thinking work but I don't do the handwriting. I invite you to watch me on my letter board and see for yourself how it is done. I have had several teachers do this. It is helpful to see I work on my own assignments, moving my own arm, and not being manipulated. I would be happy to show you any time you wish to observe.

Sincerely, Ido

Autism and Friendship
September 2011

In friendship there is give and take, easy talk, shared interests, and socializing. I see the way my sister is with her friends. I can't do what they do. I'm not referring to girl stuff. I mean the social stuff they do: talking on the phone, sports, texting, meeting at each other's homes, malls, and all the rest. How is an autistic person who is not verbal, limited in initiation, independence, and the rest, going to do that? We have an isolating illness. It stops us from doing the normal social things and it makes people want to avoid us too because we are so different and so hard to engage.

I have a few suggestions for how to be a friend to an autistic person.

- Don't patronize, even if the person seems "low-functioning." Who knows what is trapped inside?

- Be friendly and say "hi," even if the autistic person is not animated in expression or doesn't say "hi" first.

- Try to imagine what non-verbal messages the person is communicating in behavior.

- Help them stop if they get too stimmy.

- Connect in the ways you can.

I see some people are able to reach through the barrier with autistic people. They are energetic, friendly, not putting up with aggressive or bad behavior, positive and calm. The worst traits for an autistic person to be around are the opposite; lazy, grumpy, weak and afraid to set limits, negative and tense. I mean, who likes being with negative, grumpy people? But in autism we get so affected by the moods of others. I think friendship is different in autism. I am friends with people without socializing in the normal way, but I hope one day my skills will improve.

Electricity in Autismland
October 2011

I noticed that I get really nervous before I give a speech. I suppose that's normal but the truth is I felt so scared it kind of took over. I found old stims that were gone for years reappeared. My mom kept bringing this to my attention and kept saying, "Don't bring back something you overcame just because you're nervous."

She is right. It is so easy to slip into bad habits. I bothered my mom and dad with remote, non-engaged laughter. They had to struggle to get me to focus. It was like a motor car rolling downhill with broken brakes. It was not pleasant for me either.

Autismland offers an escape from my stress, but it creates stress for everyone else. I'm overly stimmy if I'm nervous, like over-charged electrical energy. How to deal with this is my life's struggle. I did get it together for my big speech. I was calm the whole time, but leading up to it I was an electrical current that was out of whack. Really I feel much better now. It is very tiring to be stuck on a current of energy. I exercised and we walked. That helped, but it is like this: I will need help either from neuroscientists or electricians.

The Lure of Stims
October 2011

In the past I internally lived in stims. The stim was entertainment, escape, compulsion, and the easiest way to deal with the frustrations of autism. It is like an alcoholic who runs to a bottle whenever he is sad or tense. It is a way to avoid working on things. It really makes the situation worse though. It is also unfair to the rest of the people who interact with the stimming person because he puts his challenges on them. In my Health class we are learning about drug abuse and alcoholism. I can't help but see a similarity in autistic stims.

In the first place, a stim is a sensory trip of enjoyable feelings. It may start small but it can take over your life. All you do feels less important than the stim itself if it is compelling. So, it is an escapist drug and it is addictive. I used to stim a lot as a young boy, especially before I could communicate. Now I stim less because I am engaged in life at a normal level, so I stay in the world as much as I can. I am thrilled about that because I don't want to live in Autismland flapping, tensing, and twirling my life away. It is hard but I am happy in school listening and learning. I may miss out on the social aspect because I don't have friends in high school—none of the disabled kids really do, I've noticed—but I do have a normal day of regular classes, and regular homework, and exercise, and so on.

But stims are there tempting me. I get stressed or bored so I return to my trusty alternative to reality. Stims are a necessary outlet at times but they have to be in moderation. If not we become drunk on them and it's too hard to return to some self control. We need a lot of help in these times and lots of activity to keep our minds engaged.

Autism and Adolescence
October 2011

Being a teenager is hard. Hormones cause mood swings and irritability. I guess it is worse in autism because our regulation of our emotions is weak. I often feel edgy and I know I am that way for nothing. It is the way I handle it though that makes a hormonal mood swing into a behavior problem. I believe I am feeling the same as all teens only I can't control my actions as well as they do. Like them I am irritable and sort of moody and impulsive. Unlike them, I can't cover it up so easily. I'm like a dog who snarls. They cuss and say rude things. I tense in my body. They bother others by teasing or bullying. It is a trying episode and I look forward to adulthood when I can feel calmer and be in a more stable state than I am now. It is a thing we all get through so I guess I have a few more years of this.

Sad in High School
November 2011

Now I'm in my fourth month of high school. I was hoping by now I'd feel at home and that I'd feel welcome there. Unfortunately, that hasn't happened. The teachers are kind enough. The students are kind enough too. The administrators are pretty eager to be rid of me. It is obvious in front of me. I can't miss it.

In middle school I was happy because the administrators were really kind. The Assistant Principal was a super easy-going man who greeted me warmly, showed me support, made me feel welcome and like the school was happy to have me there, and more. He set a tone in the whole environment, and even though my struggle as an autistic student to sit in class and control myself all day was hard, I wasn't depressed about hostility toward me and my disability. Now I am.

My start in high school was rough but it seems like it won't really get better. I am so stressed I am stimming more, aggressive more than in my whole life, and struggling all the time with fighting anger and sorrow. If I leave and I find a welcoming school I will relax immediately and I know it. Now I must focus on getting good grades and behaving well because I have goals in life and I can't let this negativity deter me. In one month it will be the end of the semester. I pray I will handle it and have a positive finish to a rough semester.

In fifth grade, I had a similar experience. When I finally got out of my remedial autism class I was sent to a school that clearly thought I shouldn't be there. It was awful in so many ways because it was hard enough emerging from a poor education and the school's attitude made it harder. So I see this attitude isn't necessary. They could be proud of supporting a disabled person who is trying to achieve a normal life. Instead they see the disabled person as an annoyance and wish he would leave their pristine campus. In a way I feel sorry for them because they limit their ability to reach out to kids.

I know I can't expect the whole world to care about me, or support me, or even like me, so I get it that not every school is for me. But I still feel sad that it is what it is. The end of the story is to believe in myself in spite of doubters. The situation doesn't make me feel like giving up, just sad that once again I have to deal with intolerance.

Struggling Against Attitude
November 2011

I live a surreal life in Autismland. I work so hard and I struggle all day to manage daily in school. I push against the door to be let in to have a decent education, but I get in and find I'm still stuck outside. What do I mean? I mean it's not easy to struggle against attitude. Maybe I need to develop a sense of humor about it. Maybe I'm too sensitive for my own good.

I gave a talk yesterday. A lot of my writings were read. In the Question and Answers at the end a nice lady asked if I really understood everything. Then after she was told yes, she incredulously repeated, "Everything?" The funny thing is, if I write smart ideas I must understand English, right? In the moment I felt mad, I must admit, but now I don't. I believe she expressed the doubt of many, actually, especially if she is a special educator or something like that. I'm sure I don't fit the model that people expect for a limited-verbal, hand-flapping oddball. Ha ha. I laugh at myself too.

I have to assume that I kind of challenge assumptions about autistic people. I have to prove to people over and over that I really am communicating. They stand next to me, or behind me, or near me, and watch me type or point on the letter board. They find I move my own arm, react to their questions, and communicate for real. How many people have I done this for? OMG, it seems like thousands, but it is only dozens and dozens and dozens and dozens...

They are professionals, and parents, and friends of my parents, and I have to prove myself to everyone so they know I am smart. I get it and I accept it. Maybe I need to get a movie of me typing that we can put on a phone and show them. Then I won't have to be observed like that. On the other hand, it is fun to see their skepticism vanish. I have sat with medical doctors, neuro-scientists, psychologists, educators, and skeptics of all kinds. After a few minutes they stop doubting and I can relax. I suppose I need to laugh, but it's the people who assume I don't communicate or don't do my own work that bug me most of all.

Thickening My Skin
December 2011

I have to aim high in life. I am the same person inside I would be if I didn't have autism. If I didn't have autism I'd be interested in a career, an independent life, and friends. I still have these goals. School is now feeling somewhat goal oriented. What I mean is, high school is a necessary step to do what I want in life. My goal is to get a college education and to work after that in education and autism, so high school is a step toward all that.

My high school is forcing me to toughen up. In the beginning I was miserable because I suspected I was not welcome. I have come to the conclusion that I really don't need to be welcome in order to succeed. Why should I worry if everyone likes me in the school or not? The truth is, I am a really visible presence because I am so different. I am somehow learning not to be a sensitive guy about this. If I am to face the whole world of special educators I better get a thick skin.

I wrote recently about how irritated I was by a woman who was shocked I understood English fluently even after I presented to an audience. To her credit she grew and learned from our interaction and wrote to me about it. That was wonderful and I give her credit for opening her mind. I was interviewed recently by medical students who were surprised to find a bright mind behind my symptoms. They were kind and open-minded and the professor told me they learned to not judge a book by its cover. Since my cover is Autismland I know some people can't see what is inside, but that is not my limitation. It's theirs.

The reality is that differences scare people. It isn't just autism. It can be physical, or cultural, or whatever. In any case, the odd man out is either welcomed by people or treated in a cold and rejecting manner. I have to realize it is individuals who are reacting to me in the best way they understand. When people have pre-judgments I must grow in my maturity. The saying is, "from adversity we get strength," so I will try to do that.

Lizard Brain
December 2011

Autism is a very frustrating disorder. I can be totally impulsive. I snatch foods I shouldn't take. I see it. I take it. No thought at all. I see things I want to spill or spray or touch. No thought at all. It is my lizard brain. It is almost reflexive. I think,—eventually—when I am caught. Then my reasoning is totally stung with remorse. I hate my impulsive actions.

I live in a dual world. On the one hand I have an intelligent mind and I think deeply. On the other hand, I only react to impulses, like a lizard chasing a cricket. Maybe neurologists or neuro-scientists can figure this one out. My whole life is extremes. I am intelligent but I am not able to speak or write like a teen. I can't even speak as well as a kindergartner. I am impulsive like a baby, but I am a religious thinker like an adult.

Autism is a wild ride. I think it is sort of a blessing to think deeply like I do, but it is so grating to follow my lizard brain as well. I wish I could figure out how to get mastery over it because people rightly get angry and I seem selfish.

Starting Over
December 2011

I went to check out another high school today. They had Open House. My high school started rough. It was pretty clear to me the school was worried about my early behavior when I was overwhelmed. It was unfortunate because I did great in middle school. Not perfect, but better each year.

In high school I started improving steadily too but I think my less than stellar start has affected the ability of some folks to see my improvement. Still, I get excellent grades and I try very hard to excel. Now I have my old, trusty, terrific aide, Cathy, all year (yay), and a new aide in training for next year. I was at the end of my rope a month ago. I came home from school in a sort of panic. I pleaded to my mom to find me another school because I felt unwelcome and she began looking and found some possibilities, but I wasn't eligible for different reasons. She found one possibility I visited today, but we don't know if I can transfer mid-year. Oh wow. It had a horse and goats and sheep, but it also had friendly people and a warm and welcoming administrator. Cross your fingers for me.

I decided to overlook the fact that I feel unwelcome now in my current school. This has helped me relax and I can see I feel calmer. It also helps me mature. Though this challenge of my high school made me grow and get tougher, I am still eager to move on to a smaller, warmer school.

Special Special Educators
December 2011

Now it looks as if I may be able to change my school. I sure hope it will be a more tolerant place. I think it will be because the tour itself was open and the administrator was kind.

I am not sure why some people choose to work with people with special needs or in special education. I would assume it would be to assist disabled people in living a normal life, in getting as tough an education as they can handle, and in some cases, even helping people. I am sure I am not unique in having many negative experiences with special educators. It is almost a power trip for some. They choose to work with people who can't fight back because they can't move or speak or whatever, then proceed to do controlling impediments that they justify as necessary.

It isn't hard to make someone feel welcome in a school. In my middle school, the assistant principal always was smiling, warm, and friendly with me. His attitude and faith in me was helpful in keeping me focused on the importance of trying. The truth is, he isn't a special educator, just an educator. Maybe that helps explain why he assumed I was just a smart kid with a disability who needed support in school and communicated in a weird way.

The funny thing is that some special educators refuse to see that, though obviously some are great and supportive and open-minded. But what about those who see the disabled kid as a pain in the butt in their school, look for behavior problems rather than focus on achievement, and seem to want failure rather than success? Why are they in special ed?

In the school I am leaving I felt a lot of negative pressure from three special education administrators who coordinated the programs for all the students with special needs, including those like me who were in regular classes. I think that they were all completely shocked that I got out of remedial education where I could be hidden. I suspect that one was certain I was not really communicating. I stopped caring because I realized it was him, not me. It was sort of sad because he had the opportunity to learn about autism but he chose stubbornly to remain ignorant. They all did.

In my opinion a school should be really proud to help a disabled person who is doing grade level work and is climbing out of a severely isolating set of symptoms. Imagine if I would be welcomed and cheered on. Then my victories would be the school's victories and I would be happy and relaxed. It didn't have to be the way it was. I am autistic in the way I see the world, but they are blind in the way they see autism.

The problem with me is that I dared to be weird and autistic and sit in regular education. This was a horror in the first degree! Someone could be injured, or the world might end, or it could give other weirdo autistic individuals the idea to get an education too.

It seems like their educational paradigm is on limitations and negative behavior, not overcoming challenges and courage, because it did take courage to face their negative energy day after day. The sort of special educators they are, are the prejudiced sort who can't be bothered to learn when a new situation emerges, but who remain stuck in old ideas, and laziness, and in a nearly cruel attitude of negativity, or worse.

Now I know I will meet these three types over and over in my life. I will meet them whether I wish to or not (not, I assure you), so I must get emotionally tough and resilient. They have earned a reputation beyond the school for being cold to special needs students, to make families stress unnecessarily, and to feel self-satisfied in doing so. It seems that the students with special needs they like are the non-special needs students. It really takes so little to be cheerful and warm and supportive to a student, and what different results can be achieved!

My struggle is to get an education and to make a difference in the world for the good, and my goal stays the same no matter how tough the fight. I look forward to the next phase in my education in a friendlier school.

The Internal Autismland
January 2012

The frustration of having autism is matched sometimes by the frustration of the parents of an autistic person. It takes so much work, perseverance, and motivation for them to fight on the bad days or moments when Autismland swallows their child whole. My poor parents say I make remote and far away expressions in those times. How I annoy others when I'm in Autismland is a problem.

Choosing to stop or escape is not always possible. My parents or aide have different strategies to pull me back to reality. I exercise or think. They make me do one or both. It helps a lot forcing me to think when my brain is sliding into sensory heaven. It is a struggle between my senses and my mind. If no one helps, my senses usually will dominate when I'm in one of those moments.

Other times I am able to get control over myself more easily. But for the tough moments, I will need lots of training and practice, as I would with sports or music skills. I notice jumping jacks help me reset my mind too. I think the one challenge is the intense OCD aspect of these stimmy episodes. It is hard to resist sometimes. It is scary too to be at the mercy of stims or impulses but I am appreciative when people persevere in helping me regain control of myself and return to Normal-Land.

Stims, Tics and Freedom
January 2012

I wish I could stop the majority of my stims. It is sort of weird to imagine my life without the stim in charge of my impulses. It is hard to explain what it feels like to people who have never stimmed, though perhaps you can imagine if you have tics or weird habits that are hard to stop. I see kids playing with their hair, gum, biting their nails. These are stim-like, though not as compelling, I'm sure. Stims are not conscious. They are relaxing, distracting, or invigorating depending on which one it is. Some are entertainment stims too.

The problem with stims is that they make me and other autistic people remote, detached, and hard to connect to. I think this is how stims are different than biting nails, for example, which is a habit. Biting nails isn't a doorway into another realm, but stims are. It is the reason why I find it hard to eliminate them from my life.

They are compelling, tempting, and easily accessed. To resist is hard beyond imagining. I think I'd love to have just one stim free day to have a respite and see what life can be without stims in it. Would it be boring or flat, or just calmer? I don't know. I guess I would quickly adjust to a new way if it was available, but it isn't as of yet.

A New Chance
January 2012

Tomorrow I start over in high school. I transferred mid-year to a new school. I was very miserable in my old high school. I got lucky. Two days before the semester ended my parents were able to get me into a new school. I think it will be a much more welcoming environment.

I wonder how my old high school would have treated Stephen Hawking, or Helen Keller, or blind mountain-climber, Erik Weihenmayer, if they had been students there. The first two were communication impaired and required one on one assistance. Helen fingerspelled her ideas and Annie Sullivan fingerspelled the lessons into Helen's hand. She was independently thinking, not writing, in her earlier years. Would she have been accused of not doing her own work? Would they have resented her noises and too visible disability? Stephen Hawking requires a lot of support. Would he have been seen as an expensive burden, or as someone worth giving the trained help he needs? Erik Weihenmayer is blind. Who knows? He might hurt himself in the busy halls, and a school can't risk that...

The reason I bring up these three amazing individuals is not to compare myself with them but to imagine how my old high school would have treated them in the years they were different, severely challenged in a big high school environment, but not famous yet. I think it is easy to know the answer. Maybe they would have decided enough is enough like I did.

Onward and upward. It is time to start over.

A Positive Change
January 2012

Every morning when I go to school I feel good now. This is like a real blessing because for five months every morning I felt like vomiting before school. I was frightened I might have to spend four years in that tension. Thank God my parents found a woman who helped me transfer into my new school. It was looking like it might not happen and it was scary because I was so miserable in my old school. This counselor did the necessary paperwork and I got in. I am so grateful to her for this. Now I have an opportunity to just learn. My school is smaller and mellower than before. The kids are more respectful of the teachers in class, and my classes are good. The great thing is the school works with my parents to make it succeed for me. They cooperate, meet, discuss, and they are nice too. I had this in middle school and again now, but for the first semester of high school it was rough dealing with the opposite. I can't understand the reason the administrators were so hostile there. The team really didn't seem to want things to work out. It is not clear to me why they had attitudes like this. I have to say I get a smile inside each time I drive by that school now and know I will never go there again. I thank all the folks who made this possible.

Exercise as a Form of Autism Treatment
February 2012

When I was a small boy I went to occupational therapy. They had me go on swings, hammer pegs, climb on ladders, and jump on trampolines. I remember one occupational therapist telling my mom that I had low muscle tone. In this case wouldn't exercise, including weights, improve my muscle tone? We worked on my vestibular processing so I went from one swing to another instead of stretching, becoming more fit, or becoming more muscular. The result is that I was not fit enough, which is a problem in a mind/body communication deficit.

Being fit enables me to tell my responsive body what to do. I work out with a trainer now because I need to have my body learn to be responsive. Now I see where my problems lie. My soft muscle tone needs to get stronger. My cardio endurance needs to improve and I need more core strength, so I work on everything. Stretching is my most necessary thing and I detest it because it is painful. I will do it because I need to and it is worth the hurt. A lot of my current problems could have been prevented if people had worked on this when I was small. I think it is essential to work on fitness and flexibility for autistic people in a regular program.

It's Not Polite
February 2012

Today I observed that I am hardly the only autistic person who compulsively grabs food. I got together with a group of autistic friends who are all non-verbal and all communicate by typing. I guess sometimes it is necessary to see others do what you do to realize it is really not okay. I tend to grab appetizing things sometimes, even if it is from someone else's plate. I know it is bad manners. I have been told this many times, but impulsive behavior is not thinking behavior. I saw that my actions are really not acceptable when I saw others do the same. One mom had a drink that looked colorful. Two kids drank from it before she could stop them. The mothers of the drinkers were embarrassed and

I thought, "I do that." Then another family arrived and in seconds the son grabbed my mom's sandwich and took a bite. Too fast for her to stop him. At first she said, "It's okay," when the embarrassed parents apologized. Then she said, "I actually don't like it when people tell Ido it's okay because it's not. I want them to correct it." The parents agreed and said that people take more offense now that their son is older, so after that my mom told the boy that he shouldn't bite her sandwich and it's not okay to take food from her plate. I think people need to do this more. My feeling is that people shouldn't excuse our bad behavior because we are disabled. When we are rude we need to be told that clearly and not enabled by understanding, polite tolerance of something that isn't acceptable. My mom wouldn't have let a dog snatch her food, let alone a human, but we tend to be too forgiving if people have autism. Don't worry. We can take the correction.

The Roulette Wheel of Life
February 2012

My dogs lucked out. All of them were rescue dogs and had a hard start in life. One is a shelter foundling, another came from a rescue organization, and our most recent find was a severely neglected, matted, starved, wormy mess my dad's cousin found in a busy street. Two came to us by chance and only one did we pick, yet here they are. I thought about this because life had a happy resolution for them. They could have died, all three, in a shelter, or in traffic, yet instead they scamper in the yard, hike, and live happy lives. They had luck in the dog lottery of life.

In life we have luck that we can't control. I mean, I've got lots of power to make my life better or worse, but not to stop my autism no matter how hard I try. That is the luck part. On the roulette wheel I got Number Autism and missed all the numbers for the normal brains. Though my chance of getting autism was low, the luck factor landed me there anyway. The roulette game is totally random. It didn't target me personally. I just had a bad deal. I suppose life has lotteries all the time. Luck is a thing I don't understand, for bad or good. I assume I never will and that no one can, but I hope my roulette wheel will decide to give me some reprieve from autism one day.

Letter to a Friend with Autism
March 2012

Dear D.,

I see that the trap of the sensory system gone awry in autism is making you sad. It is so totally understandable. When I was twelve I also felt the same way you do. In sixth grade I was really sad every day. I saw I was not easily getting better. I saw I was not having much improvement in my speech, or my hand control, or my mind body dialogue in spite of years of toil. I looked around in middle school and I saw that being different was the worst sin of all to our peers.

Like it or not, our destiny is to be different. Now I have even embraced it in some ways because I saw that hating autism made me depressed. Accepting that I could make a meaningful life for myself with autism changed everything. Inside I still wish I could be more neuro-typical in behavior. I'd talk in an instant if I could figure out how, but I feel blessed that I can communicate, even if I can't speak.

You can communicate more too if you really take it in stride. I mean it is hard to allow yourself to communicate with others after years of stimming inside. In the journey to communication you must embrace the world outside of your obsessions. I see your sensory toys. It's an incredible escape; still I see your mom wants to know you inside. Your thoughts matter to her. She misses hearing them because deep down inside you guard them so tightly. It is liberating to let go, to communicate, and to join in the world, in the regular ways of school or family. Don't give in to sorrow because we can be free in spite of the hard challenges autism gives.

Your friend, Ido

My New School
March 2012

My high school is a really nice place. The change between my current school and my old school is huge. Last semester I felt miserable, as you've read. I knew the school did not want me there. They never lifted a finger to be kind or help me feel easy or relaxed. It was so stressful it is hard to describe. The administration was really making my life intolerable when all I wanted to do was access a normal education.

The fact is, being disabled is hard enough without being rejected or made to feel awful about a disability you can't get rid of. So the difference between that kind of environment and my current school is striking. The administration is kind and happy to have me there. The teachers really are respectful of me and nice to my aide. My stomach is not nauseous when I go to school now. I feel at home, so now I can just learn like everyone else. And suddenly I no longer have any behavior problems. This is my vindication.

My realization is that the attitude of the administration is incredibly important to a school's culture. For some reason, my old school has a better reputation and is thought of as a better school out in the community. I know I'm in Honors classes so I am around the most motivated students, but my observation is that it isn't better in instruction, friendliness, or student behavior, and it certainly isn't better in tolerance of people with disabilities. The new school is like a hidden school because everyone wants to get their kids in the other one and I think this one has been much, much better. Irony, for sure.

Getting Self Control
March 2012

This morning my aide for school called to say she was sick. My wonderful dad had to turn around on his way to work and stay with me in the morning. Then my wonderful mom did the same after her meeting so he could go to work. And I had to miss school because there was no sub to be with me. I started thinking about it because I missed being at school, for once. In the past, once in a blue moon, I had to miss school because my aide was sick and there was no sub. In middle school I didn't feel too down about that because, like most kids, I liked being home. In elementary school it made little difference in my remedial education whether I went or not, but now I feel happy in school. If I miss it I feel bummed, so I got the insight that I better get more independent so I won't be in this situation again.

If I could monitor myself better I could have gone today. Autism makes us distracted by impulses, so without my aide I would stim on the way to class, take too long to sit, and be noisy. I need to be a harder worker on my self control if I want to grow into a man, not stay a boy depending on his mom for guidance all his life. The brain can triumph over many obstacles. I have read a bunch of neurology books about people with brain disorders who healed themselves somehow.

The brain is not a simple organ like the heart or liver because it has the ability to compensate or adapt to injury at times. Who can say what we can overcome or not? It seems to me I must find the way to get more self-control by resisting impulses. That is harder than I can imagine, but I guess I need to start sometime. As with anyone who fights their impulses, it gets easier with practice. But really I need to be determined to do it and I'll be honest, my determination is not consistent. The knowledge of what I must do is the start, but the fortitude to do it is the finish.

Non-Verbal Autism and iPads
March 2012

The iPad is really intriguing. Technology is helping me find a place in the world. I was liberated by my letter board which first gave me a voice. Though I have never been moved or touched when I use it, because someone else holds the letter board up, some people call it facilitation. This bugs me because it is so obvious I communicate myself that it takes bias to cast doubt. But that is the reality of being a non-verbal communicator.

The old keyboard I had was tough to use. The voice was robotic and the screen small. In more than a year I still resisted it because it was uncomfortable for me. My iPad is working out better. No one holds it. It is propped on a table. No one touches my arm, as always, and the voice is more human. I am making another transition as the technology advances.

My iPad is starting to feel natural to use. I still get a bit nervous when I am being observed or filmed, but less and less all the time. I love the game Temple Run on the iPad. I am addicted to it. I remember I used to hate games but I love this. Well, this is a lot better than forced drills of playing Candyland. Man, was that insipid. I love improving my scores and getting better. The technology is so awesome today and it helps me in life.

Progress
April 2012

I realized something interesting. Gradually my symptoms have been getting less intense. Not that I'm even remotely close to normal, but I'm a lot closer than I used to be. It happened so naturally I barely noticed, but it is true nonetheless. Very nice to recognize that it can happen. Often in the past I felt like nothing would improve and I would stay in the same situation forever.

Now I can say that I have a greater attention span by miles than before. Doing homework, piano practice, and going to school helped loads. I like playing more too. I have fun on Wii and the iPad games. I enjoy improving my skills. I see that I follow instructions better. My body listens better to my brain. The exercising I do helped here. I also have noticed that I stim less. I still stim plenty, but less. Hand flapping is way down, as are many of my stims. Instead I go and play on my iPad, which is a socially acceptable stim.

I don't know if it is because I am more mature or because I have worked hard on getting better, or both, but this gives me real encouragement to keep pressing on.

Climbing Out of the Pit

I'll conclude by saying that as I have written this book I have learned to examine my own illness and I have come to understand myself much better. When I started writing I was a bitter and self pitying person. I am not anymore. I am proud of my accomplishments and optimistic about my future. I still have a long way to go, but I have climbed high up the ladder that takes me out of the deep pit called autism. I see that I will have to work hard, but I am so grateful that Soma, and my mom, and dad, and others, helped me build my ladder out. It's not easy to conquer an illness; especially one not well understood other than by external observation. In my book I have tried to show what autism is like from the inside. Now I hope that our strange ways will start to make sense and that parents, and educators, and others, will re-examine their point-of-view. I really pray that one day all non-verbal autistic people will have the opportunity to learn communication and show the world that lack of speech is not the same as lack of understanding.

Appendix

Some Conversations on Autism between Yoram Bonneh Ph.D., and Ido Kedar

I have had a number of conversations with Dr. Yoram Bonneh, a neuro-scientist and autism researcher, about my internal language processing from a neurological perspective and other autism-related issues. Below is part of an exchange we had on this issue.

YB: You wrote that you see your words visually and spell them in your mind but that you can't say them. Does this have the quality of real speech?

IK: Yes, it has the quality of a visual version of what I think. It is like mental subtitles.

YB: How fast is this process?

IK: If I am pointing on my letter board, I hear the words in a normal conversational speed, but my pointing is much slower. If I am thinking, not pointing, it is like a visually lighting-like laser show. I hear my thoughts rapidly, though slower than how I see them. I see a lot of words rapidly. It gets overwhelming in a minute. Pointing slows down my racing mind. It helps focus my internally swirling soup of words.

I want to explain that before I could point my thoughts out in letters I understood all I heard, but my swirling soup interfered all the time with my ability to get my thoughts out. Soma taught me how to do that. The speed is a lot like a race car in a way. It accelerates if I am emotional. Sometimes it becomes a source of terror.

YB: Can you control the speed?

IK: I don't know exactly how I could control it. It goes exactly as it goes. I follow. It's overwhelming.

YB: Does it have a volume, for example, loud or soft?

IK: Yes, I hear it at a conversational volume. It is not too loud or soft. It sounds like a regular voice, however it is more a male voice than female, but really it is more of a neutral voice.

YB: Can you control the loudness of this internal speech?

IK: No, it is pretty stable in volume.

YB: Can you tap your finger in the speed of this "internal speech," e.g. a tap for every word?

IK: I don't think so. I have limited motor control. I have erratic rhythm in piano, but I'm willing to try.

YB: Can you blink your eyes for every word?

IK: That is impossible.

YB: Are the visuals and sounds in total sync or else is there a delay?

IK: It is a bit like lightning and thunder. I see so rapidly. I see letters and words. They can't be stopped. They take a lot of mental space just like a list of writing.

I hear my words behind the swirling soup. That's hard to describe. I hear it normal speed. I see it lightning swirl.

YB: What do visual words look like?

IK: They are a lightning fast swirl of lights and letters. They are my thoughts in a laser light show. Not a straight line. They move. They stir or swirl and I strive to catch my thoughts in there.

This next excerpt is from several exchanges I had with Dr. Bonneh in which I helped interpret the behavior of a non-verbal autistic student for his teacher.

YB: A child is asked to bring a chair from the other room in order to sit during lunch time and he has no problem doing it. However, when given the same request in another context, he behaves as if he does not understand the request at all. Here are some possible interpretations:

1. The child does not understand the instruction as an explicit form of language, but rather recognizes an auditory pattern that under certain conditions implies "go and bring the chair." Thus, the child is assumed to have limited language.

2. The child has good knowledge of language but this knowledge is not always available and he regresses to a lack of comprehension, as in the situation described above. This happens to me in playing the flute after a long time of not playing. I can find myself unable to play or even start a tune I used to know well, but in another time, perhaps with the help of a better context, I can play without difficulty. This type of behavior never occurs with things I do regularly, but this could be different in autism in which the cortex might be "noisy."

3. The child has good comprehension of language and understands the request in both situations, but the ability to initiate and drive the desired action depends on the strength of activation or the quality of neural representation. This representation might be at times too weak to drive the action, unless facilitated by contextual priming (as in the case of lunch time).

What are your thoughts about this? What is your opinion on a possible solution?

IK: Sometimes I really don't add it up. I mean I understand the meaning but it goes nowhere in terms of response. Then I seem like I don't understand. In situations meant to test my comprehension it was worse because I felt so terrified that people would assume I didn't know English that it interfered with my responses. It happened to me many times. Now it happens less since I communicate more. I still walk to my room every time my mom gives me a hamper and tells me where it goes. It has my dad's clothes, obviously, or my sister's, but my feet decide to go to my room. But now I can search for the right can on a shelf if I am instructed to get beans or tuna. I can do it now most of the time. It was not possible when I was younger because I didn't look or have the ability to look.

I think in the situation you describe, the chair in the new place is not as easy to see. If I didn't see something immediately I quit or just grabbed the first thing I saw even if I knew it was wrong. I don't have an answer to explain why I did that. It was awful because I knew people thought I didn't understand and I was embarrassed and flapped a lot. It happened with counting objects or handing my aunt flowers. These I wrote about in my book.

It is a weird illness and symptoms are easily misread as poor receptive language but it is poor body control, I am sure. What would help are sympathetic teachers who realize it is a body issue and who give some prompts without patronizing.

YB: Thanks for your answer. It makes a lot of sense.

I recall that another child I worked with could easily and very rapidly find a sequence of text in a page, but could not find an object in the room. He couldn't initiate the desired search movement. He even had a hard time shifting his gaze to different people in a sequence but was only able to do it very slowly, and with heavy prompting. Still, the child in the situation I described above could not see the chair in both situations, yet he was able to bring the chair when the request was made in the right context.

IK: My hunch is he had done it before in the successful setting.

YB: Could proper context assist in initiating desired actions?

IK: New environments throw off the chance of success because the body isn't able to memorize the sequence. It isn't a lack of understanding. It is a horrible body control deficit.

YB: Could holding someone's hand assist in initiating desired actions?

IK: Yes, for sure. It is like a movement opens the ability to react.

YB: Is there any other way to know that the child actually understood the request?

IK: The only other way I can think of is communication on letter board or typing.

YB: I asked the clinician who gave me the example of the boy and the chair to describe it more accurately. She said that if she told the student, "Sit on your chair," when he was next to the table he would follow the instruction more than 90% of the time. However if he was given the same instruction in a random place in the room, he would try out several different responses, and perhaps none of them would include sitting down. However he responded with 90% accuracy when she pointed to the chair. She stated that she interpreted this as meaning that this student did not have an understanding of language, but rather guessed the meaning from the visual gestures.

Is she totally wrong here? When the child was in a "random place" he could not see the chair, and according to you this is why he could not sit. But is "trying out several different responses" consistent with this explanation?

IK: I think he had memorized a series of responses that he did easily in a situation that he did every day. It became jumbled internally in a new setting in which he had no body memory. Then he did the best he could with memorized, embedded responses and she jumped to the conclusion that it was a lack of knowledge. Her pointing unlocked him to respond.

YB: The clinician adds that she usually gave her commands with a singsong tone or a particular intonation. For example she said that she told the child, "Put your hands on the table" in a particular tonality. She states, "If I told him to 'put a chair on your head,' or any random instruction in the same intonation as I normally sang, 'put your hands on the table,' he would immediately put his hands on the table. Another example is after playing a game on the floor we would sing, 'That's it,' in a particular intonation and he would immediately put his toys away. No matter what words we used, whether 'chocolate pie,' 'motorbike,' or any other word, if we sang in that intonation, he would put his toys away. She asks how you would explain that. What would an alternative interpretation to a lack of understanding be in this case? It looks like the behavior obeys the limitations of right hemisphere language as if the left "went to sleep" (or had not developed properly).

IK: It is only a guess, but here it is: he is really locked internally. His body has memorized a response to her tone or the context. If I used a phrase with you all the time at a certain time you would habituate to it. If I used special tones with the phrase you would habituate to them also. If I substitute my words you can still respond to the tone. How is it reasonable to expect someone locked internally to "put the chair on (his) head?" His body is not obeying his mind so he goes to his embedded, memorized responses.

Why is his reaction the weird one and not the expectation that he would put a chair on his head at that moment? If his teacher sings "chocolate" or "bike" in the way she would ordinarily say, "That's it," I'm not sure what she wants the child to do. Chocolate is a totally random object and it has no directions, right? It is possible he is pretty annoyed internally. Does he flap more after these tests? If he is stuck and can't show his intelligence, what is he to do to prove he understands? The prompts are her key because it enables him to react in the way she desires. I hope this helps. Tell her to try talking more normally to him. If he is like me he will be grateful.

YB: In your book you described and emphasized this motor control impairment, which affects more than communication. Although motor control and initiation of intentional actions is a major issue for you (and I believe this is generally true in severe autism), I wonder if there are other problems, such as working memory and memory recall of invisible objects.

In relation to memory, I recall a simple experiment we did with another child. We told him a single word (e.g. "cloud") and asked him to remember it. After thirty seconds we asked him to recall it and he could not. He wrote several words that appeared related to cloud, but could not get the word "cloud." We repeated this with five words, which he failed to recall after thirty seconds, but after twenty minutes he could surprisingly recall all the words. We made the obvious interpretation—that it is a memory problem. But now I wonder, could it be that he knew the word but could not type it, and could only manage to type related words? Does it ever happen that you want to type a specific word but feel unable, and can only type a different word?

IK: Yes, often. In the past my fingers sometimes insisted on some letters that they kept repeating. It is rare now. If I feel nervous it happens more. I get trapped in the letters. I need to get unstuck somehow. I think maybe this other boy was in that stuck place. In my opinion he was trying to show understanding but was stuck in a trapped spiral. He needed a break to release himself from the trap. For example, I know a boy who points all around the letter he wants but can't get himself to touch it directly. I think anxiety is a factor in this. I don't like proving my intelligence. I freak out and I get nervous in my behavior. It is a frustrating illness, let me tell you.

YB: Thanks again. These answers are very valuable.

Glossary

ABA, or Applied Behavior Analysis – is a treatment for autistic children which I did for many years when I was small. It recommends forty hours a week of in-home drills using flashcards and commands for very young children, starting in the toddler years. The basic premise is that the drills prove whether a child knows something or not, and that the way to fix an autistic child's brain is to drill and drill basic concepts until they can move on to the next level. As I explain in my essays, this really missed the mark with me because my errors were not due to a lack of understanding, but rather to my body not listening to my mind.

Adaptive P.E. – Adaptive physical education is an in- school physical education program that modifies the curriculum for students with disabilities. Often I lacked the body control to do the activities in class.

Autism – The definition of autism has evolved to include people with extreme symptoms as well as those who are borderline normal. My mom showed me a popular baby book she had when I was small that said that autistic people had no ability to distinguish people from objects, and that autistic children didn't bond to their parents, or show them any affection. That was the traditional, catastrophic view, and it likely prevented many parents from seeing autism in their affectionate children. Now, on the other extreme, some autism books label even mildly quirky people as autistic.

I fit in Autismland, and though I surely can distinguish living creatures from things, I'm much more than merely quirky. Autismland is a deep pit I am trying to escape, and unfortunately it is really not well understood yet.

Expert – When I use the term "expert," I imagine quotation marks. It is not intended to offend. It is based on my own experience. The experts I dealt with when I was young often hindered my progress because they had preconceived biases that interfered with the truth. Though I also met real experts, the many I complain about were often highly regarded by others and had a lot of power over people's lives.

Floortime – This is an early intervention which attempts to socially engage the stimming autistic child.

High Functioning Autism – This term generally refers to autistic people who talk well, have excellent body control and need less support to function in society.

Low Functioning Autism – This term refers to folks who can't communicate verbally and lack good body control. Many have not learned how to communicate because usually we can't get our expressive language out. It is often confused with cognitive delay. This is a term I dislike because it fails to take into account intellect or how well people with more severe autism can function in society with the right kind of support. According to this definition, although I attend regular high school and get excellent grades, I am "low functioning" because I require the support of a one-to-one aide.*

IEP – This stands for Individualized Education Plan and is required for any student who needs additional support in school based on a special need.

PECS – Picture Exchange Communication System is a basic level of communication system based on using symbols or pictures. A person can communicate a desire for juice by pointing to a picture of juice, for example, but anything beyond basic needs communication cannot be conveyed.

Prompt – A prompt is a hint that an instructor uses to help keep an autistic person focused on completing a task. Prompts can be verbal or non-verbal.

---

*Per this demanding standard, Helen Keller and Stephen Hawking could also be labeled "low functioning" which, based on their accomplishments, we can all recognize as absurd. On the other hand, if Helen had not been taught communication, or Stephen given his communication device, all their brilliant insights would have remained trapped inside their own heads. How easy it would be then for people to assume that they did not understand or think clearly.

Rapid Prompting Method – RPM is the method developed by Soma Mukhopadhyay which helps autistic people learn to communicate by pointing to letters on a letter board and by typing. This is how I first began to climb out of my silence.

Remedial Education – This refers to basic needs education for the so-called "low functioning" kids. This method assumes the child has cognition or receptive language disorders and therefore keeps lessons repetitive and rudimentary, year after year. In my case, because I didn't have either cognitive or receptive language delays, being "educated" in this environment for many years was tremendously frustrating.

Reinforcers – These are little rewards used in ABA for successful behavior modification. Just like you see a dog trainer put a treat in a dog's mouth for a successful trick, my ABA teachers gave me a sip of juice, or a tiny piece of candy, or a bite of watermelon, or a tickle, or a back scratch, or a high five, or a "good job!" when I got answers right in my drills.

Sensory Integration – This is a theory used in occupational therapy that hopes to help organize our senses through swings and other movements.

Stims – Stims refer to self stimulatory behavior, one of the defining symptoms of autism. They include things like hand flapping, waving strings, lining up objects, making noises, and a million other behaviors that are entertaining, fun, distracting, or escapist, but which may annoy others, and can pull us away from reality.

Made in the USA
Middletown, DE
08 August 2018